Boundaries of the Educational Imagination

WAYNE HUGO

AFRICAN MINDS

Published in 2016 by African Minds
4 Eccleston Place, Somerset West, 7130, Cape Town, South Africa
info@africanminds.org.za
www.africanminds.org.za

ISBN
978-1-928331-01-8 Print
978-1-928331-02-5 Ebook
978-1-928331-03-2 ePub

ORDERS:
African Minds
info@africanminds.org.za
www.africanminds.org.za

For orders from outside Africa:
African Books Collective
PO Box 721, Oxford OX1 9EN, UK
orders@africanbookscollective.com

Contents

Abbreviations

ADEA	Association for the Development of Education in Africa
BRICS	Brazil, Russia, India, China and South Africa
HDI	human development index
IQ	intelligence quotient
LEDC	less economically developed countries
MEDC	more economically developed countries
MiRTLE	mixed reality teaching and learning environment
MIT	Massachusetts Institute of Technology
MIT	multiple intelligence theory
SACMEQ	Southern and Eastern African Consortium for Monitoring Education Quality
TED	Technology, Entertainment, Design
UNE	University of New England
UNESCO	United Nations Economic, Social and Cultural Organisation

Introduction

The educational imagination is not free to wander and drift without discipline. It has to work with what is specifically educational, learn to push its boundaries, twist and leap within and beyond its rules in ways that illuminate. There is a discipline to the educational imagination and this book sets out to make explicit its building blocks and processes, as well as demonstrate it in action. To stretch the educational imagination means first being able to recognise its boundaries. We can start intuitively with a natural level of focus: a teacher with learners in a classroom working through a lesson. The problem is that we quickly find ourselves in a kind of Russian doll situation: dolls within dolls within dolls. It is hard to work out what the biggest and smallest dolls should be and how they all relate in educational terms. The classroom is part of a school within a district. Learners are in a grade: let's take grade 6 as a middle point. A more complex grade awaits them and a simpler grade is already completed. They are in stages of development with intellectual, linguistic, emotional, moral, aesthetic and physical dimensions that are not necessarily harmonised; and they live within different communities revolving around family and friends. The teacher is either still inexperienced in her specialisation, experienced, or an expert carrying all the traces of her own educational experiences. The lesson has its elementary components and is a part of a larger subject curriculum that is sequenced for increasing complexity. It is also located in a day that has moved from a previous lesson towards another lesson or break. At its simplest *Boundaries of the Educational Imagination* asks you to continuously move between larger and smaller sets whilst looking for connections and links. We can catch these elementary operations diagrammatically.

Dolls within dolls within dolls (figure i.1): the largest includes the smallest. The educational imagination has to learn how to climb through these levels from smallest to largest, from concrete to abstract, from particular to general, from part to whole.

Hierarchical

Figure i.1 Inclusive hierarchical levels

Dolls within dolls within dolls are linked together in complex patterns (figure i.2). The educational imagination has to learn how to negotiate the differences and inter-relationships between different systems.

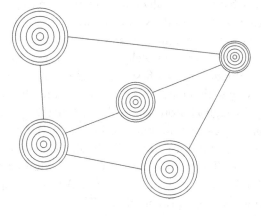

Heterarchical

Figure i.2 Different sets of hierarchical levels connected together

The patterns sketched out above continue to expand outwards, upwards, inwards and downwards. The school district expands outwards to province, country, subcontinent and continent; developing or developed region; east or west, north or south; and on a global scale. The school also exists in a space that expands outwards to the suburb, community and locality with all the complexities of class, race, gender and culture attached. The teacher brings more than her growing expertise: she has networks that operate across the grades she teaches, the subjects she specialises in, the administrative and leadership roles she occupies, and the professional bodies to which she belongs. Her pedagogy is a mixture of deep habits developed over her own lengthy period in school as a learner, the practices encouraged as she specialised in the profession and the embedded traditions of the school where she teaches. Lessons are part of the curriculum that is a part of a subject discipline with experts working at the cutting edge producing new knowledge that slowly makes its way back to the lesson in the future.

Going inwards we find that thought and language processes, and emotional, moral and bodily responses, break down into elementary units that suddenly jump to physical reactions and down to the ways proteins, cells, genes, molecules and atoms combine in a frenzied hum that we cannot hear or see across and inside teachers, learners, desks and chairs. The lesson breaks down into elementary meaning units, action units, concept units and communication units. These are built up from smaller bits that also dissolve into basic letters, synapse and sound. The lesson depends on more basic skills that go down and down into ABCs and 123s and the essential habits of the body. The simple lesson with its teacher and learners is a pulsing locus of higher and lower forces, bigger and smaller powers, longer and shorter rhythms that work slowly or quickly in intense or muted ways across landscapes riven with inequality stretching into abstract heights and emotional depth.

How to imagine and describe the smallest and largest dimensions of education, as well as its heights and depths, is the central task of this book. It is all about the development of an educational imagination. To enable this stretching, each chapter expands and contracts education through six questions:

1. What happens as we expand outwards from the materiality of one school to the collective materiality of all the schools of the world?
2. What happens when we sharpen our focus towards the increasingly smaller material parts of a school, shifting from school to classroom to desks, chairs and teaching and learning equipment?
3. What happens when we focus on the smallest functional learning components inside the body of an individual student?
4. What happens when we focus on the internal heights of development an individual student can reach on a learning path?
5. What happens when we focus on the collective heights our human species can reach on an education development path?
6. What happens if we focus on the smallest components of learning and ask how these combine to produce increasingly larger sets of knowledge?

Boundaries of the Educational Imagination starts off by taking one school and then adding more and more to the story until we reach all the schools of the world. This works by taking an already existing whole (a school) and then adding to it more and more wholes like it until a complete set of all the schools of the world is reached. The basic logic can be visualised as expanding sets growing ever larger, from one school, to schools in a ward, wards in a districts, districts in a province, provinces in a country, countries in a region, regions in the world. Figure i.3 catches the first four levels.

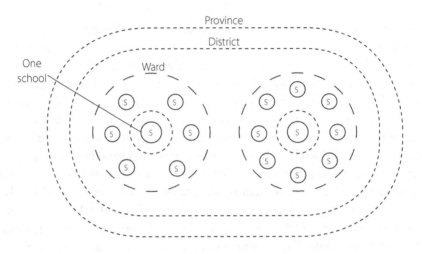

Figure i.3 From one school outwards to all schools

Second, we focus on one school and take a look inside it at its parts (figure i.4).

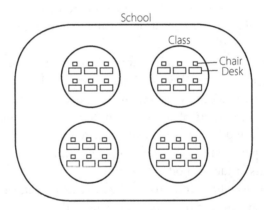

Figure i.4 From school to class to desks and chairs

The first two chapters explore the collective materiality of schooling in time and space. One way to understand what they are about is to imagine a highly intelligent alien studying our educational system from above. We can call the alien 'Tau'. Tau, From hir (his and her) spaceship, Tau can identify and track all the schools of the world as well as the human beings entering and leaving schools, but cannot come down and interview or probe us (although occasionally Tau does indulge.) What would Tau be able to say about schooling on Earth watching from above, day after day, year after year, century after century? What would Tau make of the millions of schools that suddenly mushroomed all over our planet, of the different kinds of schools in more developed and less developed countries; how we treat so many children who are not white, how we separate out those with long hair and those with short hair? The first two chapters deal with the visible mass appearance of schooling on our planet; the material collective effort of the way we educate ourselves (figure i.5).

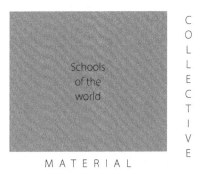

Figure i.5 The collective/material dimension of educational processes

The third chapter shifts focus from the material collective of schooling to the materiality of the individual student placed inside this massive effort. We shift from the smallest functional elements of a school (its chairs, desks and learning equipment like paper) to a learner sitting on one of the chairs and ask: what is the smallest material working unit of learning inside the learner's body? This takes us into the brain and the way it intersects with student learning. There is a difference between the fibres of paper in a schoolbook and fibres in the brain.

This signals a radical shift from desks and chairs inside the collective materiality of schools to the individual materiality of a student inside school (figure i.6). It's a massive jump into a completely different world, although each touches the other with the learner sitting inside a classroom, at a desk, writing an answer to a question with a pen.

It is hard to track the smallest material learning unit inside human beings. We have an interior inside us that is very different from the interior spaces of a school building. We have both a physical interior that is about our brains, neurons and synapses; and a mental interior that is about our minds with their thoughts, emotions and will. When we focus on the individual materiality of a student, it is hard to separate the meat of the brain from the aliveness of its functioning and that is why we use the word embodied. Working memory is our educational starting point here and the third chapter tracks how its limited capacity, dealing with around four elements at any given time, still allows for a massive expansion of learning inside us.

Education does not exist only to make us rational and productive citizens, but it has means, at its highest levels, to teach us how to reach the peaks of interior human experience. Our educational imagination cannot stop at the end of university, but has to pursue what we are at our very best and what education can do to enable this transcendence deep within our individual beings.

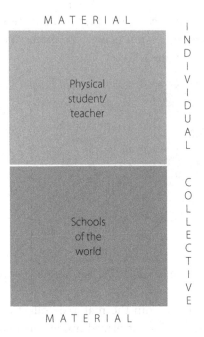

*Figure i.6 The material/collective and the material/
individual dimensions of educational processes*

The fifth chapter shifts from the interior heights and depths of an individual learner to what is happening to education at the collective level. Jean Piaget hoped that by studying the interior development of one child he could track the collective development of our species, not in terms of physical development but of knowledge. It was our collective interiority that he was after.

Those familiar with the work of Ken Wilber will recognise that the organisational base of this book uses his four quadrant model (figure i.8) and many other of his insights contained in *Sex, Ecology, Spirituality: The Spirit of Evolution*.

Chapter five asks where the education of our species is pushing us, tracking the way knowledge growth is forcing education beyond its current capacities into a new world where any one of us can access the knowledge of the world in a pedagogically structured form at any time.

This opens up the question of how to structure knowledge pedagogically. So with the sixth question we stay with knowledge, but enquire about the smallest elements of instructive knowledge. How do they combine into larger and larger groups, eventually setting up the possibility of all the elements combining in systematic and creative ways to construct a world classroom where all knowledge is pedagogically available in a smart device held in our hands?

The journey of the educational imagination takes us through four spaces: the collective materiality of schools; the individual materiality of a student; the

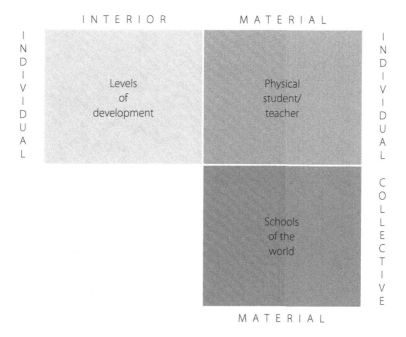

*Figure i.7 The collective/material, individual/material and individual/
interior dimensions of educational processes*

interior depths of a student; and the collective depths we have reached as a species through knowledge. It is an achievement so massive we now have to spend over twenty years of intensive education of our young just to get the basics of our own reproduction as a species in place.

But it's not just through travelling across these four spaces that we stretch the educational imagination. It's also what we do inside each of the quadrants.

At the heart of all these chapters lies the modest request to take whatever educational process or object is the focus and ask: what are the levels above and below it? How many levels can you go up and down without losing educational purchase? In this question lies the artfulness of the device: it forces you to climb up and down educational landscapes with the instruction that you stop when the levels lose their pedagogic reach. The basic modus operandi of this book is to work with what is overhead and underneath the level on which you are currently concentrating. Sometimes you will be working with the highest or lowest level, so then there are only two possible levels. But most of the time, the level of focus will have one above and another below it (figure 1.9). To become adept at using your educational imagination it is vital that you always try to think beyond the working level by going one level up and one level down, at the same time looking for equivalent elements that add richness to the level at which you are working. Level 0 is the co-ordinate level; level -1 is the sub-ordinate level; and level +1 is the super-ordinate level.

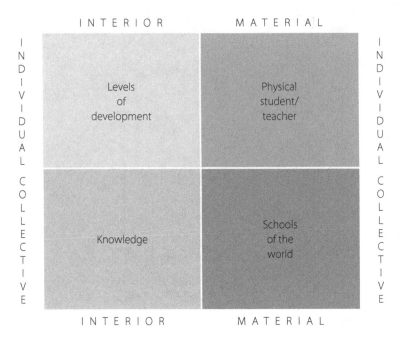

Figure i.8 *The collective/material, individual/material, individual/interior and collective/interior quadrants of educational processes*

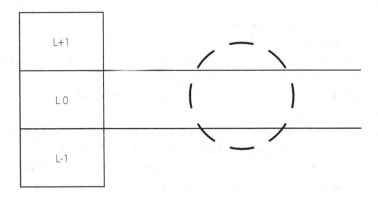

Figure i.9 *Basic levels of analysis*

You can illustrate this with the collective materiality of schools by shifting down a level to the classroom and its contents; or up a level to its location in a ward, and then you keep going from ward to district to province to country to region to continent and to the world. But don't rush the upward and downward journeys: stay with the level for a while, looking for similar and different types at the current level of focus, and practise working with similarities and differences as well as ranges of scale. If it's the materiality of an individual student that is the focal point, then start with the astonishing limitations of working memory and watch as it builds up and uses long-term memories to enable the brain to work with larger and more complex knowledge forms. If it's the internal development of an individual young learner just entering secondary school, then imagine her at the concrete operational stage but be open to developments into formal operational and the shift away from sensorimotor levels of reasoning. Then keep going inwards and upwards, if you can, beyond formal operational into more synthetic, holistic and integrating forms of logic. If it's the collective growth of our knowledge, then ask how it is that we as a species are pedagogically dealing with its exponential development, not only by looking at its largest sweep, but how the art of teaching knowledge works with its smallest units.

In summary, these chapters indicate the beginnings of ways to imagine the beauty of education using two simple distinctions: the first between individual and collective forms of education (figure i.10); and the second between material and interior dimensions of education (figure i.11; Wilber, 2000).

INDIVIDUAL

COLLECTIVE

Figure i.10 Distinction between individual and collective

Figure i.11 Distinction between interior and material

A combination of these two distinctions gives four spaces the educational imagination can travel through (figure i.12): 1– material collective; 2 – material individual; 3 – interior individual; and 4 – interior collective (Wilber, 2000).

Within each space a strict instruction is followed: climb up and down levels as much as possible without losing educational focus (figure i.13).

In the conclusion we show how this journey of the educational imagination through four spaces, using a simple hierarchical climbing mechanism, provides the groundwork for you to begin to understand the field of education studies, a field that is crucial both for the profession of teaching and the reproduction of the academy.

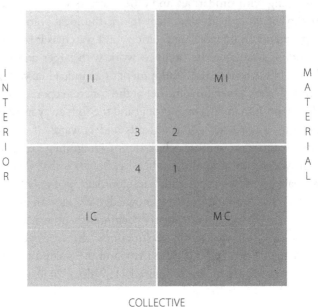

Figure i.12 Four quadrant model of educational process

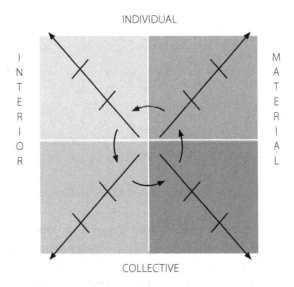

Figure i.13 Climbing through levels within each quadrant

Boundaries of the Educational Imagination is the second of a quartet of educational texts that sets out some of the basic tools needed to analyse education and develop an educational imagination. It stands apart from *Cracking the Code to Educational Analysis* (Pearson, 2013), *Conceptual Integration and Educational*

Analysis (HSRC Press, 2015) and *The Good Fight* (forthcoming), but is a sister work. *Cracking the Code* provides a simple way to take any educational object, event or process and recognise, describe and analyse what it is and how it works. *Boundaries of the Educational Imagination* takes an educational event and stretches it outwards from its smallest elements to its largest whole; and from its early and simple manifestations to the complex and profound heights it can reach. I feel this to be an elementary skill needed by anyone who takes education seriously. If you don't think through the smallest and largest, lowest and highest facets of education, then you have lessened your ability to locate where you are in the educational maelstrom and this limits your ability and imagination. *Conceptual Integration* provides a simple model to analyse and practise the transformative act of integration that sits at the heart of pedagogic practice. *The Good Fight* outlines the contested ethical justifications of education that often underlie and regulate curriculum disputes, pedagogic differences and assessment strategies, and shows pragmatic ways in which we negotiate this complex normative terrain. I mention the other three books to mark what this book does not do, so that it can do its actual job with focus and intent – take you on a wild ride to the boundaries of education and back again.

Chapter 1

All the schools of the world

It has become possible to view every single school in the world from above. Using Google Earth, you could spend a couple of years compiling a full list of all existing schools. There would be some minor classification problems around home schools, farm and village schools and some types of independent schools, but most schools in the world are obvious to the naked eye, have some kind of a boundary and a special name that can be used as a label on a map. There is a well-built and run school directly below my house called Carter High School. If I floated above my desk, high into the sky, and looked down at the school, I would see the following on an average school day:

- Around forty cars neatly parked in allocated bays;
- Tarred roads inside the school premises allowing for easy access to all parts;
- Tarred roads outside, along with wide pavements, allowing easy access to and from the school;
- A traffic warden at the main school gate every morning, directing traffic;
- Cars pouring in and out of the school from around 07h15 to 08h00 to drop off learners;
- A well-kept school with two classroom blocks and one administration block. The classroom blocks are multi-level structures with views extending over the city;
- A clear boundary that makes what is inside 'Carter High School' and what is outside 'not Carter High School';

- A massive expanse of manicured flat green fields rolling outwards from the school, bejewelled with the azure blue of the swimming pool on the one side and six tennis courts on the other;
- Repetition in many of the surrounding properties of Carter's structure in miniature: well-kept houses with pools and manicured gardens.

If I carried on floating high above Pietermaritzburg, I would see other schools and start to notice very clear differences between one type of school that looked much like Carter and a second type of a far more impoverished nature. Mpande High School comes into view. The differences are palpable:

- Fewer cars parked more haphazardly;
- No tennis courts, no swimming pool, no rolling fields, no surrounding mansions, no tarred road inside the school complex;
- Footpaths leading off from the school in various erratic directions;
- Hardly any grass;
- A permeable fence not easy to see from above whereas Carter High School has used trees and shrubs to mark its boundary with natural markers.

As I float above my district, it is striking that most schools look like the second type (Mpande). Only a few schools of the first type are around, mostly in the leafy suburbs surrounding Pietermaritzburg. As I drift outwards, away from the centre, type two schools predominate. There seems to be a split between schools clustered close to the city in the suburbs and those further away.

Very occasionally, but obviously striking, a very different type of school comes into view. Separated from the rest of the world by massive expanses of trimmed and clipped fields and long, tree-lined entrances, the privileged world of a private school (like Hilton College) unwraps itself:

- A separate community all to itself containing within it everything needed to live and learn;
- Surrounding its internal infrastructure an external expanse of forest and water, embedding a sense of tranquil isolation;
- A vast array of different buildings: a church, theatre, clinic, administration buildings, hostels, classrooms – spread out but within walking distance of one another;
- Specialised sports fields, each with a clubhouse: hockey fields with AstroTurf, cricket fields with dedicated pitches, indoor arenas for basketball, and so on.

Type one/type two across the world

You could classify the extensional set of the ten million or so schools on Earth using this technique. Viewed from above, schools would reveal their secrets in the most obvious of ways. If we imagine an alien called Tau, located in a spaceship and doing Comparative Education 1000000001, looking down on all the schools of our world, what basic sense could be made? Working only with what Tau can see of our educational system, it would be hard to avoid the conclusion that it is structured to favour the privileged few over the disadvantaged many. If Tau were in any way an enlightened being, compassion for the majority of the three billion children of school-going age would be an over-riding emotion, along with righteous anger about the injustice of it all, combined with derisory laughter if Tau knew we tell ourselves stories on Earth about education giving everyone an equal opportunity to succeed. If Tau simply and crudely classified the world's schools into type one (like Carter) and type two (like Mpande), a telling pattern would manifest itself across and within continents. A high frequency of type one schools would be found in North America, Europe, Australasia, Russia and some of eastern Asia. Type two schools would predominate in most of Africa, South America and southern Asia. This would correlate roughly with a simple map of the more economically developed countries (MEDC) and less economically developed countries (LEDC), loosely known as the North-South divide. If Tau were to draw a rough line across the world that divided it into where the majority of type one and type two schools were found, it would look something like this (figure 1.1), with type one predominantly in the North and type two mainly in the South:

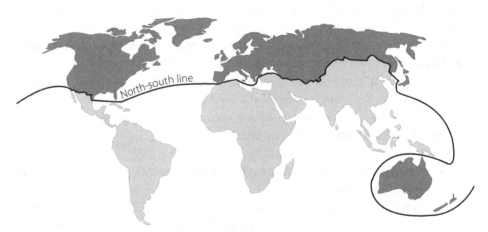

Figure 1.1 North–South dividing line

A number of other simple indicators catch the difference between these two worlds (figure 1.2). In the MEDCs of the North fewer babies are born and die less frequently, you live for longer and earn more money. In the LEDCs of the South more babies are born and die more often, your life expectancy is low and you earn very little. In MEDCs there are more elderly who are mostly well off and well skilled; in LEDCs there fewer elderly and more youth, often unemployed and existing in survival mode, or working in low-paid, low-skill jobs. In an MEDC you are very likely to live in an urban area; in an LEDC in a rural area, either trying to migrate to a city or squatting near one.

a)

NORTH

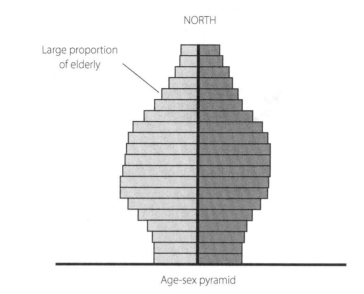

Large proportion of elderly

Age-sex pyramid

SOUTH

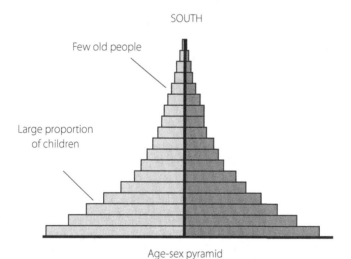

Few old people

Large proportion of children

Age-sex pyramid

b)

MEDCs	LEDCs
• High GNP	• Low GNP
• Low birth and death rates	• High birthrates
• High levels of literacy	• Falling death rates
• Export mainly manufactured goods	• Low levels of literacy
• Most people have access to safe water and sanitation	• Limited access to safe water and sanitation

c)

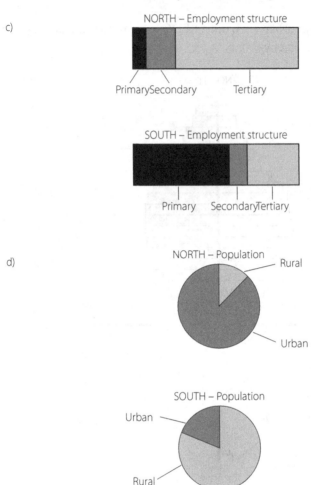

Figure 1.2 a, b, c and d: Basic differences between more economically developed and less economically developed countries

The age-sex pyramid clearly reveals that MEDCs have a larger proportion of adults in comparison to children, resulting in a more skilled population overall; whereas LEDCs have a far larger proportion of children to adults, meaning that the burden of economically bringing children to adulthood is carried by a far smaller set of adults. Notice that the employment structure bar graph indicates that most adults in MEDCs have tertiary degrees and high skilled occupations, whereas in LEDCs most adults have only a primary education and struggle to secure highly skilled occupations. So you have more adults with higher qualifications and skills in MEDCs; and fewer adults who in the main have only a primary education in LEDCs. However, if the MECDs fail to produce enough children, the real threat arises that there will not be enough economically active young adults to look after the growing elderly population expecting high levels of care.

All of these indicators correlate fairly strongly with education. The more educated a country is as a whole, the higher both gross national product and life expectancy tend to be.[1] However, it is not education we are concerned with in this chapter, but the materiality of schooling. There is not necessarily a correlation between the quality of a school building and the quality of education in a school. As human beings we can think on our feet and commit with our hearts in the toughest of circumstances: we are not bound to the conditions in which we find ourselves, but they do provide the parameters within which we work. As Marx observed in his brightest of texts:

> Men make their own history, but they do not make it just as they please; they do not make it under circumstances chosen by themselves, but under circumstances directly encountered, given and transmitted from the past. The tradition of all the dead generations weighs like a nightmare on the brain of the living (Marx, 1852, p. 277).

It is possible to enable a quality education experience in a poorly built and equipped school. There are always possible human choices and interactions in given circumstances. Nevertheless, having water, electricity, functioning toilets, desks, chairs and windows in a school helps.

As a rule of thumb, type one and two schools tend to spread across the Earth according to two spatial logics expressed in North-South and urban-rural distinctions. The North tends to have more type one schools than the South; just as urban areas tend to have more type one schools than rural areas. These two logics combine at a micro level as well. It is possible to have a division in the centre of a city between the two types of schools, just as in the suburbs, peri-urban, peri-rural and rural areas. Go into the most rural of areas and it will have its own tensions between more and less developed areas. Go into the suburbs and you will find similar divisions between more developed and less developed areas, and a tendency for corresponding types of schools within them.

It is an exceptionally crude set of ordering devices for the extensional set of schools on Earth and there are notable exceptions. But at the heart of it is an important and obvious logic that helps to understand how schooling on Earth works: the economic development of the space within which the school is located determines, to a large degree, what the school looks like from an aerial view. As Tobler (1970) noted over forty years ago in what is now called the first law of geography, 'Everything is related to everything else, but near things are more related than distant things'.

Between North-South and urban-rural

We are working with very crude logics that divide the world of schools into two simple types that work in two simple spatial ways, but it is the in-between zone that often offers the most interesting cases. Between urban and rural, and North and South, lie remarkable blends and hybrids. Take another look at the North-South dividing line in figure 1.2 and note the position of Brazil, India and China: all near the top of the bottom half and all members of BRICS with ambitions to become central players in world affairs. The danger with simple binaries is that they tend to become fixed objects rather than moving processes. The already developed North is finding, in its lack of population growth and aging demographic profile, a serious set of limitations to sustaining current living standards, initially forgotten about through borrowing but now full-blown. There are collapses downwards as others rise. That is the nature of things if you try to dominate and exploit: your time will run out and the wheel will turn.

The world is currently undergoing rapid urbanisation with massive peri-urban spaces surrounding cities. The space between urban and rural is where much movement is found; just as with the space between North and South. If it were movement that simply went from less dense to more dense, or from more distance between things to less, then we could simply stay with a ring model that shifted between a dense/close urban middle and a spreading out rural expanse. But mostly we are dealing with inequalities of relationship between urban and rural and North and South. The centre dominates, both in North and urban terms; and the periphery is exploited and stripped of its human and material wealth. The North-South division is not about different hemispheres; it is about colonialism, exploitation and domination that set up unequal flows between zones. It's a contested zone, where dominance is challenged, especially by the in-betweens. It is in Brazil, India and China that you will find some of the most extensive sets of school building programmes; and most of these schools are built in the middle spaces between the urban centre and the rural outposts.

Tau, watching from above, would note that far more new schools are being built in the strongly developing South in comparison to the holding patterns of the North.

Regionality

This logic of North-South and urban-rural divides, and the spaces in between, becomes complicated as our beautiful planet turns and school after school comes into view, shifting from Pietermaritzburg in KwaZulu-Natal to other regions in the province, to other provinces like the Eastern Cape and Western Cape if we slowly spin westwards with the sun. There are notably more type two schools in the Eastern Cape and their rhythms are markedly erratic and slow. In the Western Cape the number of type one schools increases, but something else is noteworthy: the rhythms of type two schools improve. Students arrive more quickly, breaks are sharper, fewer cars leave during the morning, and there is more activity in the afternoons. It is not necessarily the case that type two schools have erratic rhythms as some can also show highly distinctive patterns characteristic of type one schools. This provides the most intriguing of possibilities: the way type two schools can get closer to type one schools is not through what they look like in a snapshot from above, but how their rhythms work during the day. This possibility seems to be linked to the way different regions (in this case provinces) work with what they have in terms of schools and other resources.

Individual provinces have their own histories, functioning patterns and alliances, along with distinct socio-economic levels of development, so it is hard to compare how each works with schools. One way is to compare how equally poor students in different provinces perform in a standardised test. This recognises the impact of poverty on educational performance, but challenges the assumption that poverty condemns everyone equally. Individuals, communities, district and provincial structures all respond to the issue of poverty in varying ways with differing degrees of success. Take a look at figure 1.3a, which depicts socio-economic background on the x axis and scores in a standardised reading test on the y axis, producing distinct provincial profiles. The wealthier the student socio-economic background, the more to the right of the figure it will appear; the better their scores, the higher they will appear (Nethengwe, 2008, p. 94).

The Western Cape has a wealthier student socio-economic background profile than all other provinces, but notice that its poorest students are performing far better than equivalent poor students in Gauteng and KwaZulu-Natal. You can see this by drawing a straight line vertically upwards at the 50 mark on the x axis (figure 1.3b). The lowest intersection with this line is KwaZulu-Natal with students at this socio-economic level scoring around 550 on the reading score, then Gauteng with around 565 and the Western Cape high above at 600. Students at equivalent socio-economic levels perform very differently in their reading scores depending on their province.

The Northern Cape has many students who have very poor socio-economic backgrounds, but they are doing far better on average in the reading test than Limpopo, Eastern Cape, Free State, Mpumalanga and the North West. What makes the Northern Cape so interesting is not only that it has managed to produce relatively good results for poor students, but how most of its students are performing at around the same level. This is indicated by the flatness of the line, showing that students of different socio-economic levels are getting similar results. It indicates that in terms of education there is some measure of social equity, in which poorer students get a similar education to richer students.

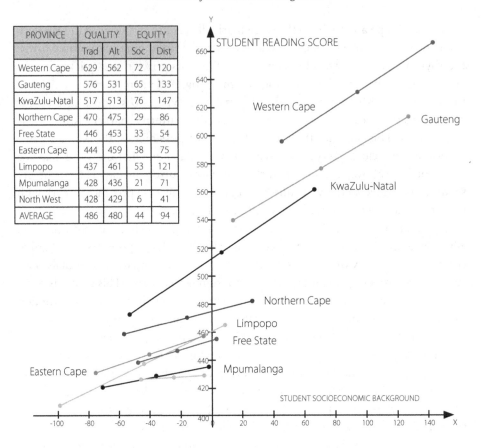

PROVINCE	QUALITY		EQUITY	
	Trad	Alt	Soc	Dist
Western Cape	629	562	72	120
Gauteng	576	531	65	133
KwaZulu-Natal	517	513	76	147
Northern Cape	470	475	29	86
Free State	446	453	33	54
Eastern Cape	444	459	38	75
Limpopo	437	461	53	121
Mpumalanga	428	436	21	71
North West	428	429	6	41
AVERAGE	486	480	44	94

Figure 1.3a South African provincial performance in SACMEQ reading test

The same cannot be said for KwaZulu-Natal where the gradient of the line is very steep, indicating that poor students are doing badly in reading and richer students are doing well. This indicates that education is not breaking the reproduction of social inequality. Rather it is maintaining the status quo, with the rich going on to university and high-paid careers, and the poor condemned to continued poverty and the battle to find adequate housing, food supplies, warmth and water. Tau, listening in to the languages being spoken at home and at school in the Northern Cape and KwaZulu-Natal, would note that there was a strong correlation between home and school language in the Northern Cape with most students able to take the reading test in their home language that was also the language used to teach at school. In KwaZulu-Natal, however, students mostly spoke one language at home and another in class. Those students in KwaZulu-Natal who spoke English at home and took the reading test in English did much better than those who spoke Zulu at home and took the reading test in English. The Zulu-speaking students, Tau would note, were also the poorest. Circling above us, Tau would weep over the injustice of it all.

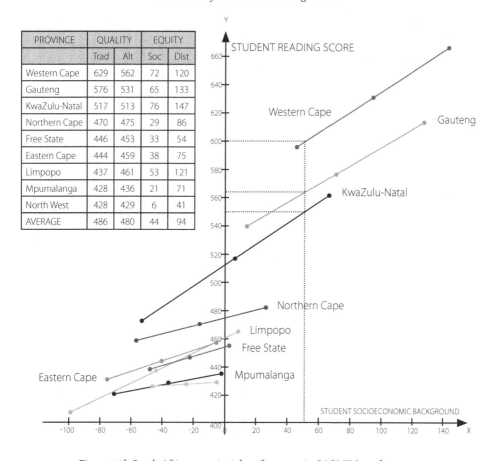

PROVINCE	QUALITY		EQUITY	
	Trad	Alt	Soc	Dist
Western Cape	629	562	72	120
Gauteng	576	531	65	133
KwaZulu-Natal	517	513	76	147
Northern Cape	470	475	29	86
Free State	446	453	33	54
Eastern Cape	444	459	38	75
Limpopo	437	461	53	121
Mpumalanga	428	436	21	71
North West	428	429	6	41
AVERAGE	486	480	44	94

Figure 1.3b South African provincial performance in SACMEQ reading test

As Tau shifted hir focus from provincial to country level, sie would see that some poor countries in terms of socio-economic level were producing good educational scores, while some relatively wealthier countries were producing comparatively bad results.[2]

Tanzania, for example, is one of the poorest countries in southern and eastern Africa. Its profile is completely on the left side of figure 1.4a, indicating severe poverty. But it is also very high up on figure 1.4a, indicating good scores on the reading test. It is producing academic results consistently higher than the wealthier South Africa. The richest students in South African public schools are performing at the same level as the poorest students in Tanzania and Kenya (figure 1.4b). Just as interesting are the Botswana and Mozambique lines in comparison with South Africa (figure 1.4c).

Students in Mozambique are almost all in a narrow poverty range with no great disparity between rich and poor, hence the short line. But notice how flat this line is. It indicates that no matter how poor you are in Mozambique, you tend to get the same quality of primary education.

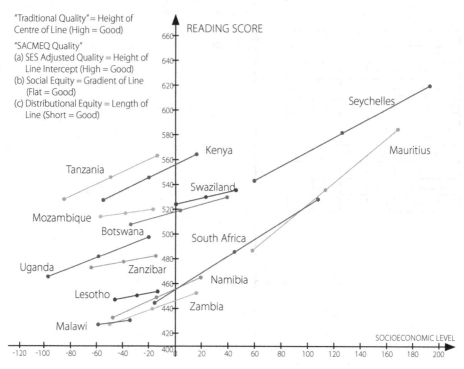

Figure 1.4a SACMEQ II comparison combining quality and equity

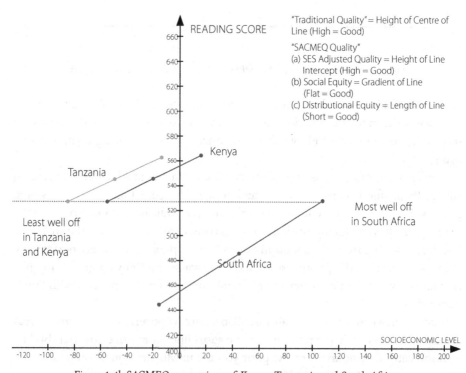

Figure 1.4b SACMEQ comparison of Kenya, Tanzania and South Africa

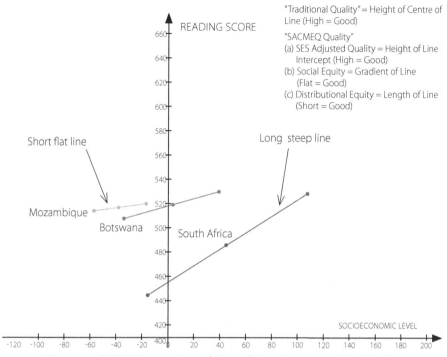

Figure 1.4c SACMEQ comparison of Mozambique, Botswana and South Africa

Botswana, even though it has many students who are comparatively well off, also has a fairly flat line. South Africa, uncomfortably, has a long line, indicating great disparity between the rich and poor. It also has a steep line, indicating that the poor do badly and the rich do well.

These test results come from the Southern and Eastern African Consortium for Monitoring Education Quality (SACMEQ) and they clearly reveal that socio-economic levels of development are not the only factors to consider when trying to improve the quality of education. If very poor countries are producing better results than more wealthy countries, then we have to focus on regional as well as urban-rural and more developed-less developed logics.[3] We can learn from our neighbours as much, if not more, than from the more developed North.

We must, however, be wary of only using one set of criteria when comparing countries. It is also vital, for example, to take a look at throughput rates from primary to high school. Mozambique has a very high level of drop outs, both in primary school and from primary to secondary school, indicating that although most of its children get a good basic education, many of them do not get anything more than that. By comparison, South Africa attempts to sustain high levels of access all the way from pre-primary to tertiary education. Many of my colleagues at universities across South Africa remark on how good African students are from across the border in comparison to local students. What is often not mentioned is how many of these African countries have deliberate policies that restrict secondary education to high performers in the primary phase, with many other learners simply dropping out; whereas in South Africa there is a sustained attempt to provide access across all levels.

So it's not only North-South and urban-rural. There are real distinctions between regions located right next to one another and this holds for localities, provinces, countries and sub-continental regions. Some schools located in both the under-developed South and poverty-stricken rural areas show regular and precise rhythms that are regional in extent, rather than urban-rural or North-South.

This gives a third ordering device that works in expanding regions outwards from a single school. Starting from Carter High School in the Umgungundlovu district (with just over 500 schools), we expand outwards to KwaZulu-Natal province (with just over 6 000) and the Republic of South Africa (48 000), escalating to southern and eastern Africa (150 000), sub-Saharan Africa (600 000), the African continent (one million); and then, the most natural boundary of all, Earth as a whole (ten million schools). At each of these levels it is possible to compare what schools look like with equivalent regions, enabling comparisons at circuit, district, provincial, national, sub-continental and inter-continental levels, providing a nested spatial hierarchy of great comparative value.

Combining regionality with urban-rural and more developed-less developed

If you are poor in South Africa and go to a type two school like Mpande, there is a very high chance that your score in standardised tests would be very low. If you are well-off financially and go to a type one school like Carter, there is an elevated chance you would have scored high in standardised tests. There are not many schools and learners between these two extremes: in South Africa you tend to go either to a type one or type two school with a sharp jump between the two. If you go to a type one school, the rule of thumb is that you do well; and if you go to a type two school, you do badly. In South Africa what counts is the school you go to: type one mostly gets you a university entrance matric; type two gets you a bare pass if you are lucky.

Figure 1.5 illustrates the point dramatically. The bar graph is split into the spread of performance inside schools (on the right) and the spread of performance between schools (on the left) and charts the differences between the fourteen countries that participated in the SACMEQ project. Seychelles has massive differences in the performance levels of its pupils within schools. South Africa has huge differences between schools, revealing the brutal history of apartheid still playing out in our system.[4]

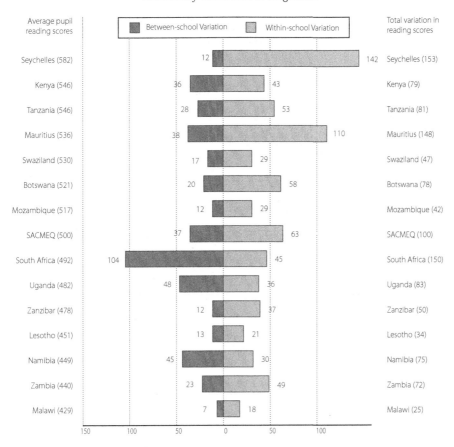

*Figure 1.5 Between school and within school variation of
average pupil reading scores in SACMEQ countries*

We can demonstrate the same point with a different set of visual representations (figure 1.6a) taken from the excellent work of Spaull (2011). In South Africa we classify schools in quintiles. A quintile refers to the division of schools into five groups: quintile one represents schools located in the poorest of socio-economic areas and quintile five those in the wealthiest areas. What is interesting about school performance in the different quintiles is that performance in the SACMEQ tests is pretty much the same for schools in the first three quintiles, with quintile five rich areas showing a massive improvement in performance (Spaull, 2011, p. 9).

The profiles of the first three quintiles all show poor reading scores with hardly any students getting beyond 600 and most scoring around 400 (figure 1.6b).

The results are not much better for quintile four schools. Quintile five schools show a radically different profile with most performing at far higher levels with a peak at around the 700 mark (figure 1.6c).

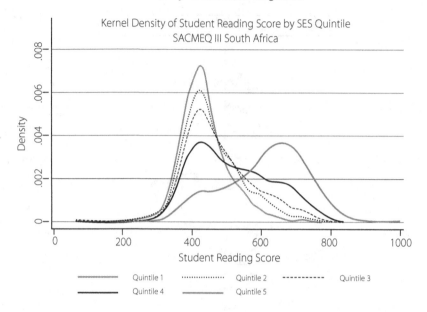

Figure 1.6a South African student reading scores in SACMEQ II by quintile (kernel density in simple terms is a more accurate type of histogram that smooth hard edges and represent data in a clear and more continuous way)

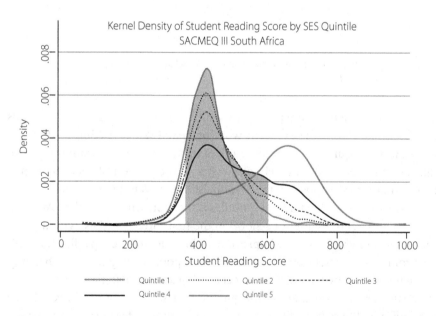

Figure 1.6b Quintile one, two and three schools all perform poorly in SACMEQ II

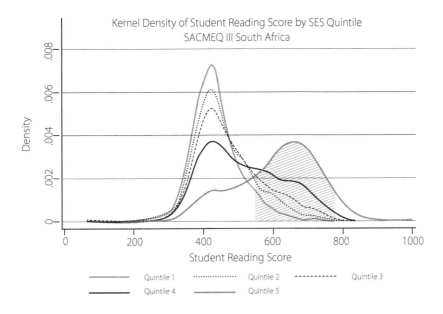

Figure 1.6c Quintile five schools perform well in SACMEQ II

If you are located in the first four quintiles, then the probability is high that your life chances will not be dramatically enhanced by education. If you are in the fifth quintile, then your chances are much better. The result is that the rich get richer and the poor remain poor, a sobering reality to contemplate. In South Africa we have a bimodal education system with the first four quintiles showing one pattern and the fifth quintile another. It is appalling that where you were thrown into this world as a baby determines your success at school. We might want to believe that education provides everyone with an equal opportunity to succeed. But the truth is a far harder reality: where you are born strongly influences your performance.

Keep this pattern in mind and take a look at figure 1.7a that breaks down student socio-economic status in provincial terms (Spaull, 2011, p. 9).

It provides a clear representation of the socio-economic levels of the students who took the SACMEQ tests, with the Western Cape and Gauteng clearly the best off and the Eastern Cape and KwaZulu-Natal deeply impoverished (figure 1.7b).

But if you look closely (figure 1.7c) you will notice that many of the other provinces sit in between the Eastern Cape and KwaZulu-Natal on one side and the Western Cape and Gauteng on the other.

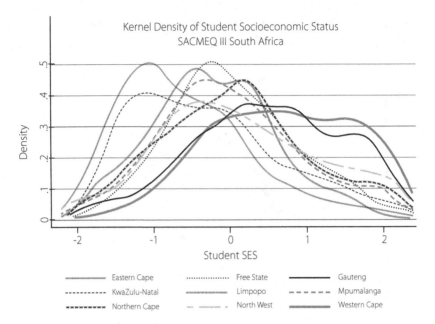

Figure 1.7a Kernel density of student socio-economic status by province

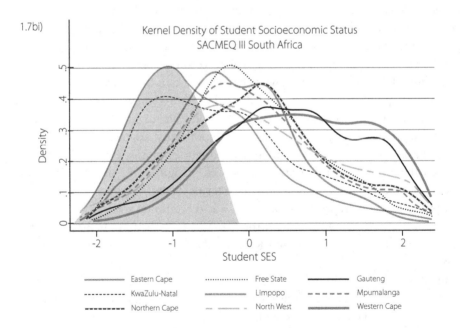

1.7bii)

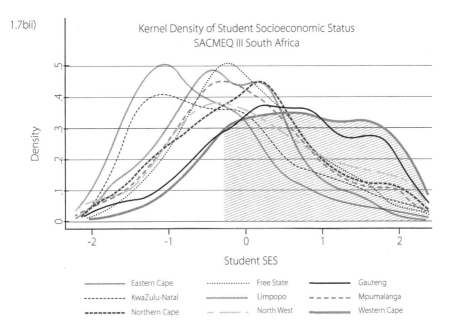

Figure 1.7b *Juxtaposition of socio-economic status of students in Eastern Cape and KwaZulu-Natal with Western Cape and Gauteng*

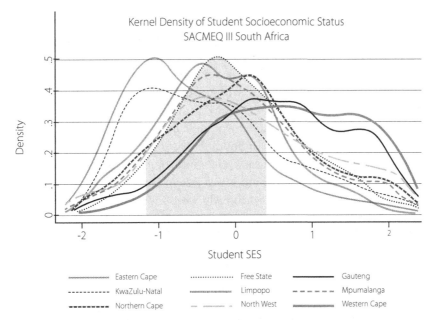

Figure 1.7c *Socio-economic status of Northern Cape, Free State, Mpumalanga, North West and Limpopo*

Now take a look at the following graph (figure 1.8) that represents the performance of different provinces in the SACMEQ III reading test (Spaull, 2011, p. 10).

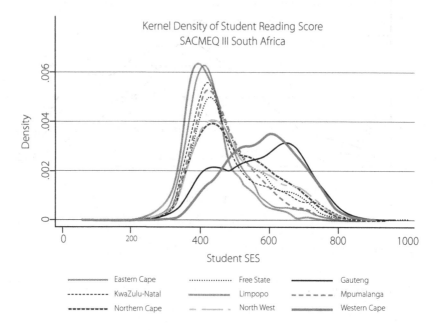

Figure 1.8 Kernel density of student reading score by province

What do you notice? What jumps out is the fact that the more spread out socio-economic status levels of the provinces sharpens into a bimodal pattern with all provinces bar the Western Cape and Gauteng performing poorly. It is similar to the student scores based on quintiles, with the quintile one to four school pattern reflected in Limpopo, Eastern Cape, KwaZulu-Natal, Mpumalanga, Free State, Northern Cape and North West; and the quintile five pattern reflected in Gauteng and the Western Cape. Schooling in South Africa is intensifying socio-economic inequalities, whether one organises schools into quintiles or provinces. Either way, the majority of students in South Africa lose out and a small minority hit the jackpot; a jackpot their parents have already won, mostly illegitimately through their skin colour or inheritance (large inheritances being largely a historical result of skin colour.)

Adding time to the spatial mix

Being an intelligent alien with some ability in Universal Comparative Education and a gorgeous computer able to keep track of all these comparisons, Tau could place them in time and observe how schools across spatial scales shift in number, quality and visible patterns over days, weeks, terms, years, or some other longer time period (physical schools pulling children into a specific space early in the morning and pushing them out later in the day began to grow exponentially across the planet about 150 years ago). Tau would see how certain schools shifted their patterns depending on what happened to the areas surrounding them.

If we spent the day observing the patterns and flows of Carter High, Mpande High and Hilton College, what would we see? Carter High School has a distinct set of rhythms. In the early morning there is a sudden major influx of cars arriving and leaving and swathes of students pouring in through the gates. This suddenly stops and hardly any activity can be seen for a couple of hours until abruptly there is a vast spilling out onto the fields and then an equally quick contraction into silence and emptiness once more. This happens twice. Two-thirds of the way through the day cars build up outside the school and the third outpouring results in numerous students, as well as some of the cars in the parking lot, leaving. But many stay on and all the fields become full of structured patterns of activity, lasting until late in the afternoon when there is another build-up of cars before the school is left empty, except for a couple of cars. The patterns are intense and swing quickly from one state to another in a controlled and predictable fashion.

Mpande High School has a less distinct set of rhythms. There are far fewer cars taking students to and from school. The main forms of transport are buses, mini-buses and feet. Students can be seen walking long distances and this continues well into the morning with a regular but slowly dwindling number of students arriving, interspersed with some leaving. Cars also arrive at school erratically, some quite late in the day, while others leave. Students can be seen wandering around the school the whole day. Like Carter High there are two periods of outflow onto the fields, but the time involved is longer and the return into school is slower. Two-thirds of the way through the day, buses and mini-buses arrive and take away many of the students while others wander off slowly down the roads. Almost all the cars inside the school depart, leaving the school quiet and empty.

Hilton College would have the least obviously noticeable rhythms from above. The only cars arriving in the morning and leaving late in the afternoon are those of teachers. There is no obvious coming and going pulse on a daily basis. Buses do occasionally arrive and leave in the afternoons, containing boys who move onto the sports fields. Activities continue into the night, with everything quietening down in this world to its own around 21h00. What goes on at night in the dorms we cannot see, although this, as well, is a world to its own.

What Tau would make of Carter High School over the forty years of its existence, by observing only extensional patterns, is fairly hard to imagine given that Tau would have knowledge of what was happening to all the other schools of the world at the same time. Two very obvious changes would jump out of this seething mass of transformations. First, the colour of the children attending the school begins to change, shifting from all white to an increasing mixture of skin colours until, eventually, white schoolchildren become a small minority. Second, there is a change from local neighbourhood children to a far more complex population, with many of the children walking down to the main road and catching mini-buses to poorer sections of Pietermaritzburg. The adults who arrive at the school to teach, however, remain mostly white and do not change their patterns, arriving regularly early in the morning and most only leaving late in the afternoon. Tau, I suspect, would love to come down to do some qualitative research to find out what was going on, but such investigations (or probes as they are infamously known on Earth) are, of course, not allowed by the Committee for Research in Universal Education across Levels, known to all intelligent species as CRUEL.

Pulsing with exploitation

But even with only an extensional set to work with, Tau would still see schools come into being, spread across the world, ebb and flow with different patterns. It would be clear that schools are not static containers for teaching and learning. The schools pulse in rhythms across all of these domains in interconnected ways that can only be understood as a relational field of various forces in competition and resonance with each other.

Pulse is a fairly neutral word. It catches the way something spreads out and contracts. But what we see happening at Carter, Mpande and Hilton is not about pulsing; it's about struggle, power, domination and the reproduction of inequality. More developed regions and countries are often in an exploitative relationship with less developed regions, resulting in power hierarchies that attempt to ensure dominance. We are not talking about regions where each does something different and relations pulse between them. We are talking about exploitation, attempted dominance and the struggle between them. Over time these struggles result in the rise and fall of dominant groups, changing who goes where and how schools function. Often it is schools caught in the transitional zones that show the most interesting shifts.

Although Hilton College has taken in more black children over the last twenty years, the way it operates has been mainly determined by its own inner logics. Mpande High, on the opposite side of the development spectrum, has not shown any corresponding increase in white children going to its classes after the revolution. It is an underdeveloped school, a situation that is very difficult to shift. But the schools caught between complete privilege and poverty are very interesting because they carry the highest charge of change in the struggle. Newly aspirant groups push for entry while already fading dominant groups are forced to consider these middle schools as downgraded options as their resources dwindle and private schools become too expensive. Tau, watching from above, can tangibly observe these changes. Tau can see the colour of learners change most at Carter, least at Hilton and Mpande; can watch the patterns of the day stay the same at Hilton and Mpande, but notice strange oscillations in the patterns at

Carter. At times, normally closer to the end of the week, term and year, patterns at Carter start to take on similarities with Mpande.

Tau can distinguish, at a minimum, five different extensional logics of schooling as the Earth continues to show its changing bright face day after day: a broad division of type one and two schools between North and South (one) and between urban and rural (two); and regional differences at different scales that complicate these broad divisions (three). As the days develop into weeks, months, years, decades and centuries, Tau can see other logics play out in the way schools ebb and flow. This gives hir a strong sense, not only of simple extensional inequality between types of schools across the world, but how they breathe, change, live and die (four). It is not only how schools pulse over time that Tau watches; but the struggle waged at every moment, across the planet, by those who have secured their place to keep it and those who have not to get it (five).

Organising buildings

Given this relational spacing of schooling, if you look carefully from above you can find buildings that attempt to stabilise different levels of scale. These are not actual schools, but buildings that house organisations working at different levels with schools. There are district offices, provincial, regional and national education headquarters, and continental and international educational buildings such as the United Nations Educational, Scientific and Cultural Organisation (UNESCO) headquarters in Paris.

The exclusivity of its architectural design as well as its location in one of the older cities of the world gives an indication of the importance of UNESCO. It has a beautifully simple but massive three-pointed star shape lifted off the ground by 72 concrete pillars. People who enter the building arrive from all around the world. Each expansion in regional level brings with it another kind of building. They tend to get bigger as the regional level expands. A district office is smaller than a provincial office that is smaller than the national headquarters that is smaller than UNESCO. There are peculiarities to this logic. Often the sub-continental buildings are far more humble than the national buildings. SACMEQ, which studies the educational performance of southern and eastern African countries, does not have its own offices and in 2012 was located in a couple of rooms in UNESCO's Harare building.

Bear in mind that SACMEQ is attempting to work with the educational systems of South Africa, Namibia, Botswana, Mozambique, the Seychelles, Mauritius, Tanzania, Kenya, Malawi, Lesotho, Uganda, Zanzibar, Zambia and Swaziland. Its scalar range is far larger than the educational headquarters of specific countries: why then its paltry allocation of physical office space?

In a similar way, the buildings that house organisations working at a continental level also tend to be more humble than either national or international buildings.

The Association for the Development of Education in Africa (ADEA) is housed within the African Development Bank in Tunis, even though it has as its focus the sharing and exchange of promising educational policies and practices throughout Africa.

It points to a curious anomaly. Organisational buildings get bigger within a country in direct relation to the number of schools under their authority. But beyond country level, this relationship shifts, especially at sub-continental and continental level, where a couple of offices often do the trick. Why is this so? It must have something to do with sub-continental and continental organisations focusing only on an aspect of education like policy or assessment; and the relatively recent (and now increasingly contentious) tendency to organise human occupation of the world at country level. District, provincial and national education levels are responsible for the actual running of schools and all the dynamics that come with it. Hence, there is an increasing need for more capacity resulting in bigger buildings as the number of schools increases. This suddenly stops at the national boundary. A different kind of focus takes over, based not on the actual running and functioning of schools, but on inter-relationships and dynamics between independent systems. And it is at this level that one can again trace an increase in building size as the institution grapples with increasing complexity, eventually reaching the global level of UNESCO. It has as its educational mission not the running and management of individual schools, but

- provision of international leadership to create learning societies with educational opportunities for all populations;
- provision of expertise and fostering of partnerships to strengthen national educational leadership and the capacity of countries to offer quality education to all;
- operating as an intellectual leader, an honest broker and clearing house for ideas;
- facilitation of partnerships and monitoring their progress, in particular by publishing an annual global monitoring report that tracks the achievements of countries and the international community towards the six Education for All goals.[5]

UNESCO does not embrace all the world's schools in the same way that a national department of education includes all of a country's schools. It cannot. It can focus on stimulating incentives and recommendations that push countries to aim for very simple targets like universal primary education. It cannot get into the intricate details of each country's idiosyncratic schooling practices, but poses clear targets for which all countries of the world can strive, possibly reach, and be measured in their attempts. These targets, for obvious reasons, have to be simpler and broader than those principals would aim for in their schools. The principal is working with a far smaller set of actants and so can focus on particularities. When your set is the world, it is best to work with what is simple and countable. Take a look at the six Education for All goals and imagine a principal being given a budget of $15 billion a year and the following list for hir performance outcomes. Make access to education equal for all children by getting governments across the world to:

1. expand early childhood education and care;
2. provide free and compulsory primary education for all;
3. promote learning and life skills for young people and adults;
4. increase adult literacy by 50%;
5. achieve gender equality by 2015; and
6. improve the quality of education for all.

Principals across the world are linked to these goals – in the end it is their schools that have to make most of them happen – but the trail from one school to UNESCO is a combination of increase in scale and decrease in particularity that puts them miles apart, both in space and function.

Education for All

The massiveness of the Education for All goals can result in a sense of impossibility, but interesting and encouraging results are emerging from the global campaign. The number of children of primary school age out of school across the world has decreased from 102 million in 2000 to 60.7 million in 2010 (figure 1.9).[6] This is an astonishing achievement given that the population of children across the world is growing. Most of this global progress is due to increased enrolment in south and west Asia, resulting in an impressive drop in out-of-school children from 37.8 million in 2000 to 13.2 million in 2010. It is clear that the struggle over the next decade will be in sub-Saharan Africa, which now contains half the world's out-of-school children and is also struggling with over-enrolment in its schools. The consequences of massive enrolment at the behest of international organisations pressurising developing states have yet to play out.

Primary and secondary education across the world

Even with these three different ordering devices – North-South, urban-rural and regional – there would be one difference that manifested itself across all regions and could be clearly seen from above. One set of schools tends to close just after noon (primary schools) and another set in the middle afternoon (secondary schools). Across the regions of the world this pattern loosely holds, but with enormous variations in the number of students attending these different kinds of school. If we watched intently from above we would see that certain countries have around

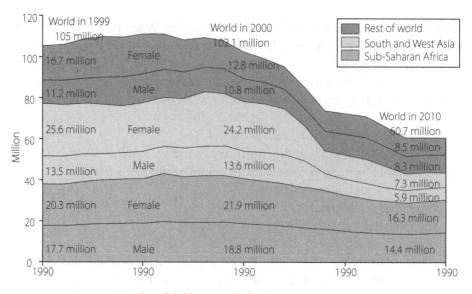

Figure 1.9 Number of children out of school across the world, 1990–2010

the same number of students going to both types of school. This would be a little hard to see initially as there are a lot more of the earlier closing schools around, but it would be offset by their mostly smaller size in comparison to the bigger and later finishing high schools. Countries like South Africa, Namibia, Botswana, Mauritius and the Seychelles show a balance in enrolment numbers between these kinds of schools (let's call this pattern of enrolment type one, using the work of Lewin, 2008)). But there are also countries like Malawi and Uganda that have very high numbers pouring into primary schools with a sudden and massive drop out from grade 2 onwards. Third, there are schools that manage a high participation rate throughout most of primary school with a strong falling away once the basics of reading, writing and numeracy are entrenched (type three). Finally, there would be those countries that simply had far less of both kinds of schools, indicating that not many of their inhabitants are going to school in the first place; and out of the set going to school not many are making it through the system (type four).

The type one pattern starts off with 100% of children ready to start grade 1 and manages, on the whole, to keep over half of them in school all the way to grade 12 (figure 1.10 – see Lewin, 2008). The type two pattern has greater numbers in grade 1 than are age appropriate, mainly because they comprise not just children who are turning six or so entering grade 1, but all sorts of others who have either failed or have started late. The result is a massive inflation of numbers in grade 1, especially if children have never been to any kind of pre-school and need a good while to adjust to the rhythms demanded by school. There is a rapid drop out rate with children leaving because they have failed too many times, they are too old, or because they need to work. The type three pattern is found in countries that have a universal and functioning primary education, but then restrict secondary education to those students who do well at the primary phase or who can afford more expensive school fees. The type four pattern reveals that much of the population is either not educated at all or receives the bare minimum before exiting the system. It is these school systems that should be targeted for massive primary school interventions (Lewin, 2008).

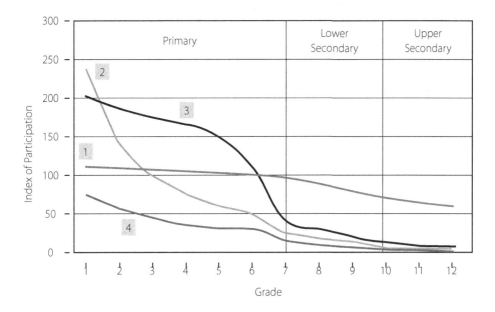

Figure 1.10 Simplified typology of enrolment patterns in school systems

Each type has a negative and positive version, with the percentage of students still at school in grade 12 the defining criterion. Some type one systems are able to keep the line astonishingly even at around the 100% mark, meaning that all their children are going to school and managing to progress all the way through the system. Some type two systems start with serious over-enrolment, but then flatten out and sustain a healthy pass rate close to the 100% mark for primary school and only fall away in high school. Some type three systems sustain participation strongly into high school. Some type four systems have a fairly low enrolment rate, but at least keep these students all the way through school, ensuring that the portion of the population starting education also goes on to finish it.

Watching the number of students in primary and high schools across the world from above would show up some crude patterns. Western and central Africa would show a mix of negative type four pattern with low enrolment and high drop out or a negative type two enrolment pattern with over-enrolment in the very early grades and then a severe drop out rate. Some areas in south Asia would show a positive type four pattern with low enrolment and low drop out. Latin America, in the main, has a negative type two or type three pattern, with high enrolment in primary school and then rapid drop out by the time of high school. East and central Asia, North Africa and southern Africa have a negative type one pattern with high, even enrolment and a late but fairly substantial drop out rate. North America, Europe and some parts of east Asia have a positive type one pattern with high, even enrolment all the way through. Lewin (2008) provides us with a simple device to classify all the education systems of the world according to how many students each system carries successfully through the grades.

Tertiary education

What happens to students after grade 12? Again, if we stayed with the view from above some of the students land up going to a very different looking set of educational institutions with a notably distinctive set of patterns. The whole rhythm and look of tertiary institutions is different from primary and high school when regarded from above. Here is an aerial view of my university's campus.

The boundary is far more porous and buildings are more varied than those of schools. Students and cars come and go all the time, and there are more cars and parking lots than in schools with many students stealing lecturers' parking spots. There are always students milling about from morning to night and it's hard to tell who is a student and who is a lecturer as they both dress equally badly. There is a notable correlation between urban areas and tertiary educational centres, as there is between North and South with the North having far more tertiary institutions of greater size than the South. At a regional level there are also notable differences, with countries like South Africa having more tertiary institutions than all its neighbours put together, indicating that more of its students are achieving higher levels of education. Observed from above in conjunction and over time, primary schools, high schools and tertiary institutions reveal that educational institutions cover years from early childhood to adulthood and change their rhythms and outputs based on age cohorts as well as their location on a North-South, urban-rural and regional basis.

One result of the Education for All drive has been the massification of higher education as more and more students pour from secondary schools into tertiary education. There has been a wide range of responses to the increased demand for tertiary education, with innovative responses around distance programmes as we shall see in chapter 6, but this surge in demand has also produced highly problematic effects. Many African universities, colleges and technikons are struggling with the pincer of increased enrolment and static or reduced funding, resulting in increased workloads for lecturers, rapidly deteriorating infrastructure and a drop in the quality of delivery; and increasing student frustration with overcrowding, broken down residences, and inadequate library and computer facilities. To survive, many African higher education institutions have been forced to run separate programmes for students who did not qualify for state bursaries or subsidies. The universities charge the full economic cost of running these programmes to the non-funded students, thus gaining another stream of income. This means lecturers are forced into double time work for students who are often under-qualified, resulting in a dumbing down of the curriculum and devaluation of tertiary qualifications (Mohamedbhai, 2009). This pattern is only going to intensify as Education for All plays out its logic into an under-resourced and over-stressed tertiary sector.

What would the whole world's profile of primary, secondary and tertiary education look like, and how is it changing? Tau would be able to keep track of this simply by counting how many students are in all the primary and secondary schools and tertiary institutions of the world, and then trace what happens over the years. Tau could go back in time, use the patterns shown to extrapolate into the future and report back to CRUEL where the world will be in 2050. Some promising earthlings (Samir et al., 2010), aiming for universal CRUEL bursaries, have done similar research and here are some of their early results. Taking the auspicious year 2000, they produced educational attainment projections for 120 countries (93% of the global population) that go back to 1970 and forwards to 2050. This would be interesting in its own terms, but the results become fascinating when the interplay of education, fertility, mortality and migration are considered. Higher education is strongly correlated with decreasing fertility, lower mortality and increased migration. This allows future demographic predictions based on current trends.

The first step is to prepare a country-by-country database of the age, sex and educational profile of populations with the millennial year 2000 as the baseline. Most of this information is available from the United Nations. Four education categories are used: 'no education', primary, secondary and tertiary. You then divide the population up into five-year age groups and keep track of sex differences as this is key to fertility rates. Then think of an elegant and simple way to represent the data visually so that mere mortals (especially politicians) can understand it. Give each education category a different shade, with light aptly chosen for no education and dark for tertiary education. Put males on the left and females on the right. Run the age groups upwards from 15 to 100+. Here is South Africa in 2000 and 2050 (figure 1.11a and b).[7]

It's a pedagogic artefact of considerable beauty. South Africa is destined to become a country that has eliminated the 'no education' category, that has more women than men tertiary graduates, and has almost reached universal secondary education (rather than primary education) as its goal. This results in the pyramidal demographic structure shown in 2000 bulging outwards and upwards as birth rates decline, migration to South Africa increases and mortality rates decrease.

How does this profile compare to other countries? The profile of Singapore (figure 1.12) taken from a similar study that tracks what has happened to its population in terms of primary, secondary and tertiary educational attainment since 1970 and projects where it is going to by 2030 for males and females.

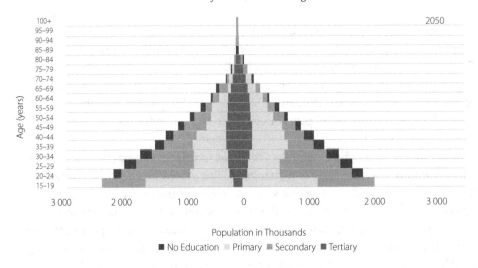

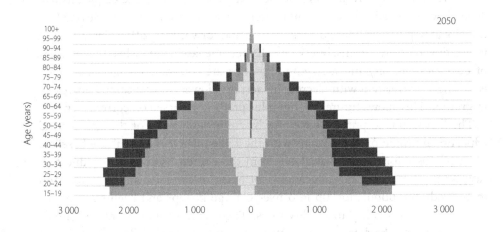

Figures 1.11a and b Comparison of education levels for South African population, 2000 and 2050

A great deal of information is contained in figure 1.12. First, note that Singapore's population is expanding quite rapidly, not because its 15–19 year group is growing, but because all the older groups are living for longer and immigration to Singapore has been strong. Second, note that much of its population was uneducated in 1970, especially amongst the older groups, but this has increasingly diminished: by 2030 it is projected that everyone under 50 will have a basic primary education. Third, note how rapidly tertiary education grows, resulting in a projection in which by 2030 almost half of Singaporeans under 60 will have a tertiary education. This is becoming almost mandatory in some countries and is seen as a major strategy to enable a competitive outstripping of other countries in the development race to the top. Unlike many African countries where massification of higher education means over-enrolment in a system already at bursting point, with no substantial increase in funding in sight nor ability to increase gross enrolment much beyond 5% of the national population (Mohamedbhai, 2009), countries like Singapore are making higher education a national priority. The aim is to have over 50% of the population qualified at tertiary level.

What makes the Singapore story so useful to this chapter is not only the contrast with what is happening in many African countries, but how it is breaking out of a national into a transnational model of tertiary education. Along with other countries in the Asia Pacific region like Hong Kong and Malaysia, Singapore has turned itself into a regional hub of higher education by attracting top universities from America and other Western countries to set up campuses and then encouraging students from across the region. All sorts of organisational models have been researched, experimented with and implemented. Some universities offer almost exactly the same curriculum in Singapore as at the home institution in the USA or Britain, others set up models more appropriate to the Asian context, while yet others offer joint degree programmes in conjunction with local Singaporean universities. And this does not only apply to universities: private schools and colleges have also been encouraged to open their doors to the business of learning. Higher education has become a transnational industry in Singapore.

Division of the sexes

If Tau contemplated our schools from above, not for a day, week or decade, but over the last two hundred years, another set of patterns would become obvious. First, Tau would note that the building of schools only began in earnest two centuries ago, but since then has shown ever-increasing growth.[8] Second, Tau would observe that initially there was a strong division of the sexes, with boys and girls either going to different schools or split into different sections of the building and playground when attending the same school. Third, Tau would realise that over the whole of the nineteenth century only white children from the North attended school throughout their childhood, with a rapid spread of this practice from the North across the world only in the last 120 years. Tau would also observe that initially the education of white and black children was kept separate and that this only began to change very recently. The global obsession with attendance of all our children at schools is recent and still shows the scars of its Northern, urban, white, male history.

We can see this clearly by using a nineteenth-century text that went on a grand tour through Europe and America. As Robson charts for us the changing shape of schools and classrooms across the Western world in the nineteenth century, he closely observes the different kinds of school arrangements for the sexes.

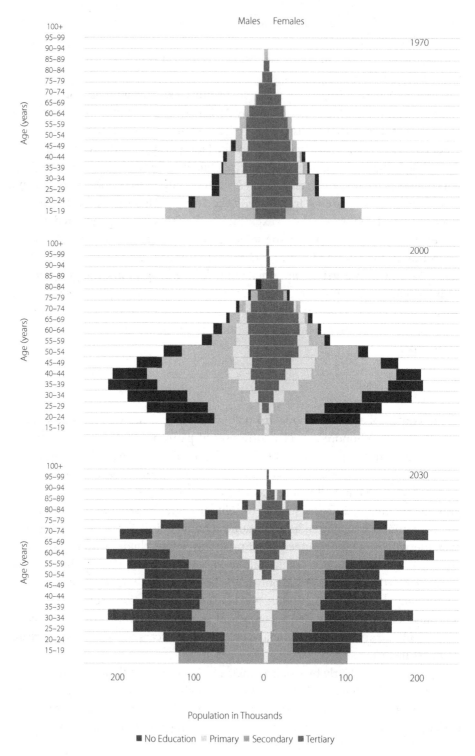

Figure 1.12 *Comparison of education levels for Singapore population, 1970, 2000 and 2030*

Unlike English schools that tended to keep boys and girls separate, many American primary schools taught the sexes together, but split the classrooms in half, boys on the one side and girls on the other. Punishment often consisted of being sent off to spend time in the opposite half. Another option was to split the building in two, with a boys' half and a girls' half (figure 1.13), each with separate stairs and playgrounds (Robson, 1874, p. 31).

Watching the schools of the world from above, Tau would have seen the sexes either split off into different schools or playing separately in clearly demarcated sections of the playground. Tau would have noted that there were clearly more boys' schools than mixed or girls' schools. And if Tau happened to drift over any of the bureaucratic buildings responsible for the administration of schooling, Tau would have seen mainly white men entering the buildings. This would have stayed the same even when women increasingly took over the actual teaching, initially dominating elementary schooling but slowly spreading upwards to secondary schools.[9]

Another strange pattern Tau would have observed concerned certain regions in the East, which suddenly increased the number of girls in schools by the middle of the twentieth century. Communist governments in Russia and China made equality of education an explicit goal, resulting in the rapid inclusion of girls in mass schooling. Tau would also note that in certain countries exactly the opposite happened with girls suddenly disappearing from schools in countries like Afghanistan due to the radical fundamentalist demands of groups such as the Taliban.

Floating above us over the last two centuries Tau would also have observed massive differences in the ways white- and black-skinned students were schooled. What we observed happening in Pietermaritzburg as we panned out from the beautiful, historically white school just below my house to Mpande High is a theme throughout the world. Black children, in the main, receive an inferior education in inferior buildings compared with that of white children. Only in the 1950s did America break away from the practice of housing black and white students in different schools under the pretence that it was possible to have separate but equal educational structures. It took South Africa another forty years to reach a similar conclusion that separate is not equal. Unfortunately, conclusions don't change material reality very easily.

Contemplated from above, all the schools of the world reveal key configurations that can only be ignored by the most blind of species. A massive fissure runs between North and South: some of the worst schools in the North seem luxurious when compared to the South. As it tears the world in two, it is necessary to work first with this divide before beginning with any other type of inequality. It highlights another fundamental division that can be clearly seen from above: the quality of schools in urban areas compared with rural areas. To go to school in the South in a rural area and be placed in competition with students from the urban North is simply a travesty. The dream of equality of opportunity is simply that; a dream

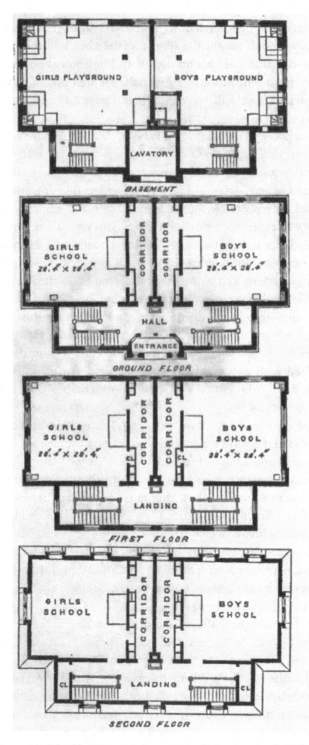

Figure 1.13 School building and playground split into boys' and girls' sections

that one needs to be asleep to believe. A third division palpable from above is how different regions, even within the North-South and urban-rural continuum, pattern their schooling. Some regions that are mainly rural and South show very different patterns of schooling to their rural and South neighbours, revealing crucial logics that get beyond the fatalism often connected with extreme divisions and inequality. A fourth type of partition revealed from above is that between types of school for different ages of students, caught by the division into primary, secondary and tertiary institutions. The urban North tends to have a healthy carry through with students attending educational institutions from a very young age until their early to mid-twenties. The rural South shows up very different patterns with both a strong drop out rate and increasing lack of schooling infrastructure as the age level increases. This general picture is nuanced with a more regional view that shows how different regions caught in the same South-rural knot work very differently with the problem, providing hope and insight in dealing with tangible inequality across the world. There is a reason why South-South exchange has become a key driver of new knowledge and network formation. You see the differences of those closest to you most keenly and feel their successes with an acidic bite, because it takes away many of the excuses for your own failure. If they could succeed in a similar context why can't you? All these differences are yet again cut through by tangible variations between the education of white and black, and male and female, students. To pursue these geographic insights an excellent place to start is the superbly illustrated *World Atlas of Gender Education*.[10]

I do not doubt that an intelligent and empathic alien watching us from above would weep at the way we conduct ourselves with our young, but there are some indications that we are slowly improving how we materially deal with our own reproduction. We are building new schools every day, bringing more of our children, whether they be boys or girls, black or white, rich or poor, urban or rural, North or South, young or old, into schools for longer than ever before. There is a general upward trajectory tracked and encouraged by international and national organisations and policies. It gives a little succour to the disgust that can arise when circling above the schools on our planet, especially when combined with the rank smell of pollution poisoning our planet.

Chapter 2

Unpacking classrooms

It is hard for Tau to observe the material contents inside a school from an aerial view. To get it right the school would have to take all of its material artefacts outside and place them on the field. We could then observe what each school contained. Desks, chairs, curtains, overhead projectors, books of various kinds, smart boards, computers and other technical equipment, posters, models, and musical and sports equipment could all be laid out. Telling differences would quickly emerge between schools, much as Peter Menzel found when he went around the world photographing the possessions that different homes contained (Menzel, Mann and Kennedy, 1994). To get all the possessions of an American family in range he had to hoist the family up on a cherry picker and put all their possessions in the background. Even so, the photograph left out many of their possessions. Contrast this with a rural village in Uttar Pradesh, India, where the full set of belongings of the Yadev family (including food, cooking equipment and furniture) came to less than 20 items.

Menzel produced another book about what families across the world eat. He asked families to place in front of them all the food consumed in a week. The photographs are tragic to contemplate. A family in Chad smile at the camera with only the barest necessities placed in front of them (Menzel and D'Aluisio, 2007, p. 56) while a German family have stacked to overabundance in front of them beer and bratwurst along with healthy doses of fruit, vegetables and bread (Menzel and D'Aluisio, 2007, p. 133).

The North-South, urban-rural divide is a tangible one: you can touch its pain and taste its excess. It is from these different kinds of home that children go to school. The German and American families had lots of books in their possession, whereas the Indian and Chadian families had none, except for a single religious text. Tobler's first law of geography, 'Everything is related to everything else, but near things are more related than distant things' (Tobler, 1970, p. 236), would lead us to predict that something similar would happen if we had to display all the furniture and equipment of schools close to these families: massive piles of equipment on the school fields of Germany and the USA; and just some desks and chairs in rural India and Chad.

What would we notice if we unpacked the different rooms of a school into separate piles on the field rather than one pile in the middle? Would we be able to see what the different rooms do based on what they contain? A library and computer room would quickly reveal their functions, as would most audio-visual rooms. Art rooms and science laboratories would also quickly reveal themselves, as would the medical centre, staffroom and hall; sports, domestic science and technical centres; and possibly even the furniture of the principal and deputy principal's offices and reception. But as we floated above the fields from urban to rural and from North to South it would also become painfully apparent that some schools have only the basics and that all their different rooms seem to contain much the same stuff: desks and chairs in the main, often maimed or broken. Specialisation of function would be hard to determine from classrooms' material contents.

This would become even more painfully apparent if we had to unpack the contents of the most privileged private schools. This was brought strongly home to me recently when I visited one of these schools to talk to the teachers about what distinguishes an excellent teacher from a good one. As I walked down the tarred internal road, there were signs pointing off either side to buildings, each holding a specialist function – sanatorium, museum, chapel, theatre – mostly prefixed with the name of some illustrious retired headmaster or former student turned benefactor. The administration block was a two-storey building, as large as some schools, all on its own.

Note what we are doing in terms of the educational imagination. Instead of moving spatially outwards to more and more schools and the expanding spatial logics this wide-angled focus gave us, we are now focusing on the school itself and how it works, with its classrooms, desks, chairs and pedagogic equipment giving us increasingly smaller levels inside the material reality of a school on which to concentrate.

One classroom and one teacher per school: the Lancasterian way

If we went back to the early 1800s we would find plenty of debate around what a school should actually look like. Western industrialising countries had not settled on what a school should be, or on what classrooms, desks, chairs, and writing and teaching equipment should be. Take the blackboard we find in many classrooms around the world. When blackboards first arrived at schools they had to be argued for. Many teachers resisted them, found them impossible to understand and use and could not see the use for them. Blackboards were not obvious pieces of equipment and it took a long time for their use to become entrenched. There is a wonderful little manual produced in 1841 entitled *The Black Board in the Primary School*. It contains a homily to 'the very simple and incomparably valuable, though much neglected, appendage of the schoolroom, the black board' (p. vii). The writer of the homily bemoans its lack of use to a clergyman on one of the school committees and this was the response given: 'No,' he replied, 'it is of no use to get them. If we had black boards, we have no teachers that can use them to advantage' (p. vii).

I can resonate with the sentiment, not with blackboards but with our own modernised version – smart whiteboards. We acquired one for our university's school of education. It literally sat around like a white elephant, and was eventually used simply and tragically as a board to write on; tragically because the red marker used was of the cursed permanent ink variety.

Back in early nineteenth-century England it was not even clear that there should be classrooms in a school. Here is what a typical Lancasterian school (figure 2.1) looked like at the beginning of the 1800s (Lancaster, 1810). There are no classrooms, only a schoolroom for all the children, no matter what their age. The dots represent school children sitting in long benches, divided into 8 'grades'.

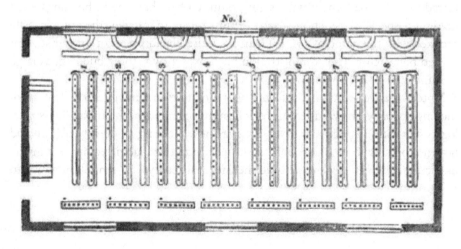

Figure 2.1 Lancasterian school plan

If you packed everything outside you would have twenty long desks and benches, a teacher's desk and chair, slate tablets and slate pens for each boy and a lesson board for each row. There would also be printed arithmetic books; paper, pens and inkstands for the older boys; and sand desks, plus an alphabet wheel, for the youngest to practise finger writing. There would also be badges of merit and disgrace marks made of wood to be hung round the necks of children, pointing sticks for monitors, a bell, a whistle, a clock and some books for a library (British and Foreign School Society, 1816, pp. 5–11). That's it for a whole school of around three hundred boys. How did they do it?

All the boys were housed in one schoolroom (figure 2.2a). Different ability groups were divided up into rows with long benches and tables for each group to sit and work. Once you learnt the curriculum for your row, you could move back a row (even if the others in your row had not matched your performance) until you reached the back row and then possibly graduated to being one of the pupil monitors on the side, assisting a particular row of boys. Boards were hung on the side walls to allow the monitors to teach and question. The boys were allowed to gather round their own particular board in a semi-circle (2.2b).

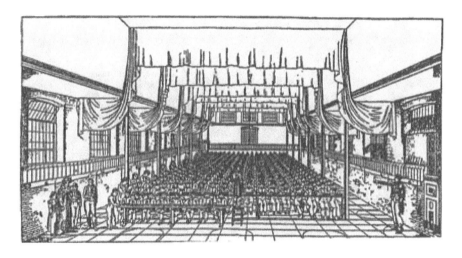

Figure 2.2a One schoolroom – no classrooms

The teacher presided over proceedings from a raised platform at the front of the room. Around three hundred boys at different levels could be taught in one room at the same time (Burke and Grosvenor, 2008, p. 39).

Lancaster begins his book, *The British System of Education*, with the image shown in figure 2 .3.

No. 3.

Figure 2.2b School monitor with boys from one 'grade' in semi circle around him

Figure 2.3 Frontispiece

Lancaster explained the frontispiece to the book as follows:

The monitor is represented standing with a pointing stick in his hand, to enable him to point out the best performance, without touching the writing on the slate, which might accidentally obliterate the writing.

The boys are represented as sitting in the first desk in a class, in common with which they are exhibiting their slates, at the command from the monitor

"SHOW SLATES!"

They are represented as having written not merely a word, but a sentence; and a sentence that every true Briton will wish to be engraven, not only on the memory, but on the hearts of the rising generation, as a tribute of duty to the monarch, who reigns in the affections of his people —"LONG LIVE THE KING!"

Slate tablets were cheap, fairly easy to maintain and could be wiped (Hall, 2003). The materiality of slate enabled and afforded a particular type of pedagogy. First, it was cheap, so it enabled the spread of mass schooling. Second, it enabled visibility as all the boys would have to display what they had written to the teacher or monitor. This forced attentiveness as any mistake or lag was quickly picked up (Hall, 2003). Third, it afforded repetition and practice as each response could be quickly wiped off to enable a new one. Fourth, it allowed for simultaneous teaching and learning. As the teacher spoke, so the boys would write, reinforcing what was heard with physical action. Fifth, it enabled continual activity by all the boys at the same time without wasting materials. Finally, it afforded continual movement of the boys up and down the rows depending on the correctness of their responses, enabling a competitive meritocracy to motivate performance and attention. Paper and quill pens were expensive and difficult to procure. Continual maintenance of the pens was needed and much ink was spilt, literally. This resulted in the increased use of slate tablets and slate pens during the nineteenth century until mass production of pens and paper took over.

Military precision was needed to keep all the boys learning at the same time. Here are the duties of the monitor-general when using slates for dictation:

Duties of the monitor-general before dictating begins

4th. When the children are seated, he gives the command in a quick, distinct, and audible tone of voice – *Unsling slates*. The children catch the string belonging to the slate with their left hand and with the right they hold the slate and place it on the desk.

5th. The next command is *Clean slates*.

6th. After the slates are sufficiently cleaned, the monitor-general gives a signal to leave off by ringing a bell. The pupils then place their hands on their knees.

7th. He then orders them to *Show slates*. The boys cross their arms, and taking the upper corners of the slates, raise and turn them in such a manner that the clean side is seen by the monitor-general.

8th. His next command is *Monitors, Inspect*. The monitors leave their places and examine the slates of their pupils to be certain that they have cleaned them well. They then return to their places, and turn the telegraph to show the general-monitor that the inspection is finished.

9th. His next command is *Lay down slates* after which he rings the bell as a signal on which the boys put down their hands.

10th. He then directs the Monitors to *begin*. The monitor of the eighth class dictates a word; then the monitors of the 7th, 6th, 5th, 4th, 3d, and 2d, in succession (British and Foreign School Society, 1816, p. 49).

This sets up a continual cycle of writing, showing and cleaning.

Compare this to the modern slate currently making its way into schools, the iPad and its various (cheaper) tablet rivals (figures 2.4 and 2.5).

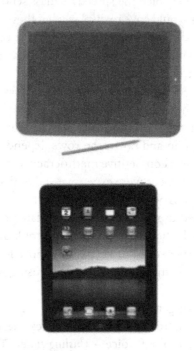

Figures 2.4 and 2.5 Old and new slates

The development of technology when contrasted like this over two hundred years is genuinely astonishing, but we do have to be careful. The Apple iPad is very expensive, needs to be continually charged and has to be carefully looked after as damage is often fatal. It freezes, crashes, needs continual updating, is prone to attacks and viruses, and can be used as a portal to worlds into which young learners simply should not go. At present it does not afford the same possibilities for mass education as a slate tablet. The iPad is not as robust, easy to use, tangible, cheap or safe as slate. These are crucial considerations when thinking about mass schooling. It is also the case, however, that modern technology (here I am thinking specifically about mobiles – smartphones and tablets – that have cameras, GPS, web 2 capabilities and apps galore) contains within it the dissolution of modern mass schooling as we currently picture it.

It is hard to see at present because there is both hysterical hype from tech evangelists about the revolutionary potential of new technology and a failure to understand that education is about far more than technology. That said, something about Marshal McLuhan's aphorism 'the medium is the message' rings true about mobiles. Not only can all textbooks for all years be downloaded and continually updated on a tablet, condensing the school satchel that I lugged around into one small device, but it can also hold all the writing books, tests, homework, projects done over the years, and keep track of them. It can serve as a school notebook, art book, calculator, GPS, maths tutor and video player – the list goes on and on. The teacher can keep track of every single student on hir (his or her) own device.

But this is still keeping within the traditional school paradigm. The mobile enables continual real time interaction with anyone who is also connected, anywhere and at any time, fundamentally breaking the materiality of classroom walls. It spins knowledge out of the control of the official curriculum with a little expectant blank box and search button. YouTube contains brilliant lessons on every conceivable subject, often performed more successfully than by actual teachers in actual classrooms. More than this, it is now malleable, with students able to take it and manipulate it into forms they prefer, share it with whom they like, and develop reference groups that spin way beyond their teachers and class peer group. It condenses time and space into one gadget, breaking away from the necessity to have a specific place for schooling at specific times with a specific age group. I can imagine defenders of slate tablets getting a little tetchy at this point and pointing out that slate tablets can also be multifunctional: 'What about the slate tablet combined with calculator that has been around for hundreds of years and doesn't ever need to be charged?' they might say. And they would be right: there is such an object (figure 2.6) and it is a beauty to behold.

Figure 2.6 Abacus and slate

A school with classrooms and teachers

But we have moved very quickly from the materiality of early mass schooling in England to its future dissolution. What of the two hundred years in between? What makes the Lancasterian set up so strange for us is the absence of different classrooms for different age grades. Most of us experienced school in the physical space of a classroom where we were divided up and separated off in age bundles. This was by no means the obvious way to organise schooling in nineteenth-century England. When the English architect Robson undertook a grand tour in search of the best schools in Europe and America in the 1870s, what impressed him was the Prussian school system. He notes with both excitement and surprise that 'The system in use among the whole German speaking race ... turns on the theory that each class should be taught in a separate room by a separate and fully-qualified master' (Robson, 1874, p. 12).

Imagine that! All the discussion in English education about whether the schoolroom should be wider or narrower to accommodate all students, or about how to work with pupil-teacher monitors, is absent from German debates because they don't have one large schoolroom, they have classrooms in a school, and they don't have children teaching other children, but qualified adults teaching them. What an idea. Is it not obvious that you need pupil-teachers, given that adult teachers are expensive, and that you need to work in a large hall with small groups that are continually checked and monitored, rather than small classrooms with only one teacher struggling to keep control? What could be wrong with a plan that shows how one master without any other teachers 'might conduct a school of 1 000 children with perfect ease; and that while their progress in learning was much more rapid than in the old method, the expense for each child need not, in a large school, exceed 5s. or 6s. per annum' (British and Foreign School Society, 1816, p. iii). Don't laugh, though. Our current debates about the size of classrooms and pupil teacher ratios will look equally strange by the turn of the twenty-first century.[11]

Robson was enormously impressed by the German classroom and the manner in which it had been developed, given its one-hundred-year head start on England over mass schooling. It was the Prussians, not the English, who embarked on mass compulsory schooling in 1763.[12] It had become clear to school architects in Germany that classrooms as a rule should not exceed a length of 30 feet and a width of 21 feet, with a height of no less than 13 feet. The reasons for these particular dimensions are fascinating. First, the Germans insisted on all the windows being to the left of the children, ensuring that the right hand did not cast a shadow whilst writing (Robson, 1874, p. 84). There was no electricity, so in effect the width of the room was determined by the amount of light reaching the desk furthest from the window along with an extra three or four feet for a gangway.

This meant that the width of the room could not be more than one and a half times the height of the room (Robson, 1874, p. 85). The length of a classroom was determined in part by how far students could read writing on the blackboard and by how far a teacher's voice could reach without straining, both estimated by experience to a maximum of around 30 feet. Furthermore, the breadth of a classroom should not be more than 21 feet 'because then pillars or complicated construction are required' (p. 84). Each child should be apportioned three square feet, anything less being unhygienic with a maximum of sixty children per class. The size and shape of the classroom was not arbitrary in any way. Its spatiality was not at the whim of the architect or school planner. The materiality of the classroom in its own particular functioning asked for a certain length, width and height. As Robson notes after lovingly describing a number of German gymnasiums, 'the old idea, now forever exploded, was that any kind of building would do for a school, and that the shape of a barn was as good as any' (p. 117).[13] Ditto for the classroom.

Light and air – in search of the elements

The fascination with light in classrooms was not a peculiarly German preoccupation. There are grounds for claiming that it has been the central visionary organising device of classrooms since the project of mass schooling spread in Europe more than two hundred years ago. The School on the Sound, Copenhagen (1937), for example, attempted to maximise natural light, fresh air and closeness to outside surroundings by creating massive window/doors that opened out to allow inflows from the outside (Burke and Grosvenor, 2008, p. 81). The walls could be folded back, creating a feeling of being in the open air whilst still being protected from the elements. Children with exposure to the elements would be healthier children, tougher children, fitter than the rest children; able to survive war and hardship, able to be hardy citizens and, if the time came, hardy soldiers. Public health, hygiene and racial superiority pushed the desire for light and air to the extremes of open-air schooling. The French League for Open-Air Education argued that exposure to the elements would contribute to the

> [r]estoration of the French race, fight against tuberculosis, alcoholism and the causes of degeneracy. Raise strong and vigorous generations. Train well developed, active determined young men and women; men who love their country, are ready to serve and defend it … women who will conscientiously support their husbands, housewives who are attached to their home and prepared for their social role (Burke and Grosvenor, 2008, p. 82).

These visionary attempts to provide more and more light inside the classroom fell foul of their own absurdity, impracticality and expense, and the continued endurance and replication of the older stock of schools with their rectangular classrooms built from brick and mortar.

Virtual classrooms

Some classrooms do not have to exist in brick and mortar form – they have mushroomed in virtual reality as well.[14] Virtual worlds such as Second Life make it possible to create interactive, computer-simulated environments in which students can learn. These simulations create a virtual classroom space that mimics a real classroom with chairs and desks and student avatars sitting in place and responding to the teacher. These classrooms can be used to train teachers, just as we use virtual machines to train pilots and truck drivers. For an example of a virtual classroom see the one created for pre-service teachers at the University of New England (UNE).[15]

You enter the classroom with an avatar that can walk, speak and interact. You have control over what your avatar looks like. Sue Gregory and Yvonne Masters, two of the lecturers on the virtual reality course at UNE, have their own avatars respectively called Jass Easterman and Tamsyn Lexenstar, and as a teacher you can choose who you would like to be and what you look like. Students enter this virtual world and engage with the avatar lecturers, other students, the environment and the task. As useful, immersive and engaging as this second world is, most students still prefer real, live interaction with actual people. But the problem with real live interaction is that it is expensive, happens only in one time and one place, and must be repeated year after year; whereas Second Life is cheap, and can happen across time and space.

Simulated worlds are shifting quickly from a gaming environment across to education, real world activities, and back to gaming. Driving simulators, for example, are used to train truck, train and bus drivers. It is much safer to simulate a crash situation for a driver to respond to and experience the consequences of her decisions, rather than have the actual crash. As simulation improves to the point where the participant feels like she is really in a moving vehicle, it has produced all sorts of unexpected results, one of which is simulator adaption syndrome (SAS). A simulator can make you feel as if you are in a real situation, but there are enough differences to cause driver discomfort. Simulators often react to driver responses in ways slightly more delayed than real time, resulting in many drivers developing motion sickness, headaches or disorientation.

This can carry over back into the real world, where the real car you are driving suddenly feels very strange after a couple of hours of simulated driving experience. A friend of mine almost wrote off his car when driving home after playing a racing car simulation game (Grand Turismo) at my house late into the night. It is an immersive game with a steering wheel, gears, brakes and accelerator that gives you physical feedback (the steering wheel shakes and resists). Different cars can be chosen and racing specifications can be altered, resulting in distinct effects actively experienced in the drive. On his way back home he took a corner too fast and almost wrote off his Golf. It did not handle in quite the same way as the virtual Ferrari he had been driving for a couple of hours. What is astonishing about the effect is that the game did not cost the $15 million dollars it took Toyota to develop an immersive driving simulator; it cost under five thousand rand and can be found in middle-class teenager rooms across the world.

Although classroom simulations have not reached this level of virtual realism, there are increasingly sophisticated attempts to virtualise classrooms as we saw with the Second Life example. The most sophisticated current attempt at a virtual classroom that I know about is simSCHOOL, started up by David Gibson.[16] It is a classroom simulation that has a number of artificial students, all of whom have different characteristics, needs and learning styles. As you teach the class, student responses shift and change and you have to work out what responses work best both for individual students and the class as a whole. At any stage you can check how your individual students are doing and at the end of the lesson a detailed report is given of the effects of your decisions. You can go back and try again to improve your performance and learn through the process different instructional strategies, classroom management techniques and relationship building with students. You can also design your own classroom with your own unique students and your own lesson, and share it with other teachers and teacher educators across the world, building a dynamic online community all engaged in improving teacher education. But even this kind of virtual classroom does not get close to what is going down in medical education.

In medical education there has been a long history of using simulation, now reaching the point where students practise medical procedures on plastic, real-life, computer-linked models that respond according to the student's actions and provide invaluable practice and feedback in skills such as suturing, anaesthesiology and minimally invasive surgery. An intern learns to respond to a crisis during the birth of a baby, not on a real live baby but on a baby mannequin set up in a true-to-life situation. This has resulted in specialised medical simulation centres that set up hospital environments, often to high levels of fidelity, with mannequins that have human-like tissue density and can do things such as adjust bleeding, pulse and blood pressure levels.

The United States army also has simulation centres, only these work with scenes of battle. A medic has to work quickly and efficiently under enormous pressure with a range of injured mannequins as smoke, bullets and explosions reverberate, making decisions and performing actions depending on the state of the mannequin. All of this is recorded on computers, enabling analysis of and feedback on the medic's performance.

Moodle and MiRTLE

As the demand for education increases, and distance education becomes increasingly popular as a way to address this need, the combination of virtual and actual classrooms becomes attractive. Universities and schools across the world have embraced eLearning as a crucial dimension of teaching and learning. Learning management platforms like Moodle and Blackboard are not as spectacular as simulation machines, but they provide tangible benefits to students. Moodle, for example, at the end of 2014 had over 66 million users and over 7 million courses.[17] It allows a lecturer or teacher to set up online websites for students enabling all sorts of information, documents, assignments, quizzes and discussion groups. Students can submit their assignments and receive feedback online, discuss issues with other students and the lecturer, and download all the documents and files related to the course. Lessons are still face to face, but many of the other activities surrounding teaching and learning are enabled in a virtual world.

This combination of students being taught in real physical classrooms while also engaging in virtual space has increasingly resulted in the blending of different realities. It has now become possible to include distance students in a real time lecture, not just by allowing them to watch the lecture from a remote location, but by having them present in the actual lecture. This is called a mixed reality teaching and learning environment (MiRTLE).

In the physical classroom lecturers will be able to deliver a lecture in their existing manner but they will have the addition of a large display screen mounted at the back of the room that shows avatars of the remote students who are logged into the virtual counterpart of the classroom. Thus the lecturer will be able to see and interact with a mix of students who are present in the real world or the virtual world whilst delivering the lecture. Audio communication between the lecturer and the remote students logged in to the virtual world is made possible via a voice bridge. An additional item of equipment located in the physical world is a camera placed on the rear wall of the room to provide a live audio and video stream of the lecture to the virtual world.

> From the remote students' perspective, they log into the MiRTLE virtual world and enter the classroom where the lecture is taking place. Here they see a live video of the lecture as well as any slides that are being presented, or an application that the lecturer is using. Spatial audio is employed to enhance their experience such that it is closer to the real world. They have the opportunity to ask questions just as they would in the physical world via audio communication. Additionally a text-messaging window is provided that allows written questions or discussion to take place (Horan, Gardner and Scott, 2009, p. 5).

The dimensions of a classroom worked out in Germany over two centuries ago are beginning to shift, as is the very idea that classrooms form the spatial unit of teaching and learning.

No classroom classrooms

Whether actual or virtual, the idea of a classroom has established itself firmly as a basic organising unit for education. To see how firmly, take a look at the following story taken from rural KwaZulu-Natal and told by Costas Criticos:

> The school, which is bursting at the seams, always has one class which finds itself without a classroom. These classes have to go out to the dusty playing field for their lessons. You might expect … that the teacher and class would seek out one of the few shady trees as a refuge from the harsh sunlight. Instead of this, the class filed out to an area in the middle of the playground where the floor plan of a classroom had been neatly marked out with stones. The 'classroom' even had a break in the wall for a doorway. The children stood along the wall of their 'classroom', while the teacher who was standing at the 'doorway' waited patiently for them to get into a straight line before she gave the command to 'go in'. The class didn't walk through the virtual concrete block wall, but instead, turned deftly in through the doorway and made their way to their neatly arranged rows of 'virtual desks' (Criticos, undated, 4.1–4.2).

Criticos was stunned by what he witnessed and muses over what he saw: 'What is so attractive about the classroom and the rituals played out in these spaces that teachers and pupils are conditioned to regard them as normal? Why does the classroom become the organising unit on which development proposals are based?' (4.2).

He concludes that the 'traditional teacher-centred classroom as the basic unit of currency in education is overvalued and in need of examination' (Criticos, undated, 4.2). It's not so clear to me that this is a failure of the educational imagination. Teachers understand the need for ritual as the core musculature that holds a school together. To shift away from a classroom-based model would result in all sorts of disruptions to the way things are normally done, and these disruptions would foreground themselves rather than allowing the lesson to emerge in its own right. It's not easy to create a space of taken-for-granted actions and habits that allows a zone of concentration to open out from its tacit ground. The best way to do this is to keep as much as possible of this world in place, precisely to allow for the space of the imagination to unfold. The virtual classroom in the middle of the playground with its imaginary desks and chairs is a double victory for the educational imagination: first because it holds the rituals of classroom life in a hostile space; and second because this provides students the tacitly-given rituals they need to engage with new knowledge.

The furniture of teaching and learning

Concern over getting the ergonomics of school furniture correct is not a peculiarly recent phenomenon: it has been with us from the beginning of mass schooling. As Robson travelled around the Western world chronicling the materiality of its school architecture, he also provided a detailed account of how different countries were responding to the need for desks and chairs that worked pedagogically, but were also cheap and simple to manufacture. In his simple, direct, but deeply insightful way he notes:

> It is yet a feature seldom thought of at the outset, and not until the building is finished and ready to receive the furniture, is it found how much more suitably the schoolhouse might have been planned had the desk question been first decided. Too frequently the complaint is similar to those so commonly heard against the houses run up by speculative builders, in which the bedroom has no proper place for the bed (Robson, 1874, p.168).

Speculative builders have not changed their habits. Is it possible to say the same of our children and how they sit and learn at school? Granted, children have become larger in the last 150 years with longer arms and legs resulting in a current re-evaluation of the dimensions of school chairs and desks, but has anything substantially changed in the material design of what children sit and write on for around thirteen thousand hours of their lives?

The first difference quickly jumps out. A major design issue of school chairs and desks in the nineteenth century was the need to ensure comfort 'not for sitting at or for standing – but for both' (Robson, 1874, p. 169). The choice for our modern children is whether to sit or lounge, not sit or stand. Apart from this, school furniture designers struggled with a multiplicity of issues. Should there be long benches and tables, or tables and chairs for two children, or just for one child; should the table and chair be designed as one unit, or separately; should it be fixed to the ground or not; and should the desk have a flap for storage, be foldable for stacking and cleaning, adjustable for different demands? As always, there were designers who were enamoured with designing the best possible desk and chair that could do everything for everyone, but never made it in the mass schooling market where cheapness and simplicity are prime movers.

For example, Herman (2011) tells the story of early twentieth-century attempts at designing a 'modern' school desk combination in Belgium where almost every single joint was adjustable to enable children to find their own sweet spots. These were simply too expensive to mass produce and too finicky for mass everyday robust use, and were abandoned for simpler, cheaper, robust models. The twenty-first century is no different, with a continual stream of sophisticated and adjustable school chair/desk combinations falling foul to the twin requirements of affordability and durability.

There are, however, some key differences between the sophisticated early twentieth-century designs and current models. Ergonomic research has increasingly recognised the need for an open posture when sitting at a desk, meaning that your body is stretched outwards to a more upright position rather than hunching over the desk. The angle between torso and thighs is extended from less than 90 degrees to 135 degrees; the health benefits of which are research proved (Dennehy, 2009). Contrast this to what standard school furniture expects of posture: the hunched back effect. Schoolchildren tend to try to get their heads within 30 centimetres of their work and will sustain peculiar positions for long periods while writing and reading (Dennehy, 2009, p. 13). Why not start from scratch and design school furniture that takes into account what we currently know is best for posture and concentration? Why not increase the height of the chair to enable a more open posture and tilt the desk to prevent hunching, rather than force most of the body into a contorted form of dormancy that has given me my characteristic hunchback look. Why not encourage an active form of sitting that results in a strengthening of inner core muscles rather than a slow descent into weakness and fat? All I know is that whilst writing this my thighs are extended less than 90 degrees and I am hunched over the keyboard.

Keep it simple, stupid

The difficulty with these excellent designs is that they collide with the demand of mass schooling for simplicity and parsimony. When working with millions of desks and chairs, it is vital to keep both costs and the possibility of breakage down. Only when new designs are able to go to scale and are robust enough to withstand the attentions of a bored teenager, might they stand a chance of gaining a foothold in the world of school furniture.

Robson knew this many years ago. He reserved some of his most cutting remarks for school promoters and desk manufacturers who 'render what ought to be one of the simplest articles of school furniture a species of harlequin, capable of assuming a new character at a moment's notice. When too much is attempted, the result is never satisfactory' (1874, p. 170). A harlequin is a comic character in plays dressed up in colourful clothes who never does a simple movement but always embellishes with a cartwheel or a flip. Now that's an insult worth bringing back into our post-modern repertoire.

So what did non-harlequinny desks and chairs look like in the nineteenth century? One option was to combine the desk and chair, not only as you would imagine from the front, but from the back (figure 2.7; Robson, 1874, p. 367).

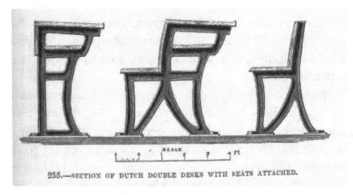

255.—SECTION OF DUTCH DOUBLE DESKS WITH SEATS ATTACHED.

Figure 2.7 Dutch double desks with attached seats

This arrangement worked for either double desks or longer benches. The problem with the above design is that the seats are not moveable, making it harder for the student to enter or stand and difficult to clean around. Moveable seats (figure 2.8) answered these problems.

This did not solve the issue of the visibility of the child to the teacher: 'in grouping the class the object is to enable each child to see the teacher, and the teacher to command the face of each child' (Robson, 1874, p. 75). This was especially a problem for students at the back, resulting in a strong focus on raising the height of the back rows, either through sleepers on the floor or increasing the height of the desks and chairs, or both. Take a look at the following two solutions (figure 2.9) and try to work out which solution is better.

Remember that it is always simplicity that carries the day when working with mass education. The top option is a simpler design than the bottom one, with only one step, not two, and all but the last row having the same size desks. Most teachers preferred an even simpler option, a flat floor, and this is what has prevailed in most classrooms around the world.

The dual desk system also brought with it specific drills for entering and leaving (figure 2.10). At the end of a lesson the teacher would issue the following six orders: 'return', 'slates', 'lift', 'desks', 'stand' and 'out' (Robson, 1874, p. 377–378).

The students would then be ordered 'quick march' and march off with left foot first. You don't need Foucault to get the intimate connection between military discipline and schools.

So what did the twentieth century bring to the mix? Invented in the mid-1960s, the monobloc chair (as it is technically known) was in mass production in the 1980s, with a single press able to take two and a half kilograms of polypropylene and mould it into a chair in less than 70 seconds.[18]

Initially, just the seat and back were produced by injection moulding with the metal feet added manually, but by the 1980s designers had worked out how to vary the strength and thickness of various parts of the chair, enabling the far stronger but still light full plastic chair we use today (see Parsons, 2009, pp.

264.—AMERICAN DOUBLE DESKS WITH SEATS ATTACHED.

Figure 2.8 American double desks with seats attached

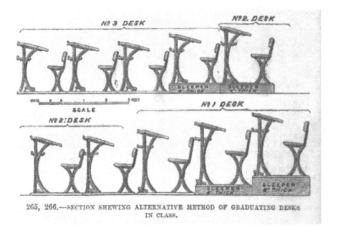

265, 266.—SECTION SHEWING ALTERNATIVE METHOD OF GRADUATING DESKS IN CLASS.

Figure 2.9 Section showing alternative method of grading desks in class

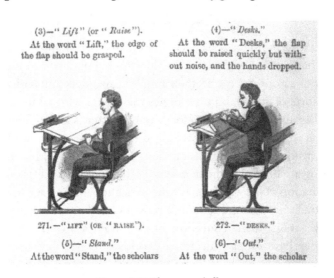

(3)—" *Lift* " (or " *Raise* ").

At the word " Lift," the edge of the flap should be grasped.

(4)—" *Desks.* "

At the word " Desks," the flap should be raised quickly but without noise, and the hands dropped.

271.—"LIFT" (OR " RAISE").

272.—"DESKS."

(5)—" *Stand.* "

At the word " Stand," the scholars

(6)—" *Out.* "

At the word " Out," the scholar

Figure 2.10 Classroom drill

100–102 for a brief history). Its virtues are that it is inexpensive, lightweight, washable, weather-proof, stackable, airy and comfortable. Its vice is that once it breaks it is only useful for landfills where it does not biodegrade and sits around with millions of other plastic chairs sharing the same fate whilst millions more pop out of presses every year. The plastic chair embodies the peculiarly modern quest to turn whatever possible into a fully automated industrial process (Sudjic and Brown, 1988). Combine this with a trapezoid table (figure 2.11) that can be laid out in various group work and individual arrangements and we have the stunningly beautiful classic combination of modern school furniture. How far we have come.

Figure 2.11 Plastic chair and trapezoid table

Take a breath for a moment, look back over the first two chapters and ask what the journey has been trying to do to your educational imagination. We started with a single school as our focus and then rapidly expanded outwards and travelled through all sorts of space and time logics that come with taking all the schools of the world as our object, looking for tangible patterns and differences. We then turned around and instead of travelling outwards we went into the school to see what it was made of, again tracing how the internal working of the material dimensions of a school played out in time. The intent behind this whirlwind trip down imagination road was to get your educational mind-set to shift from its focus and attachment to the here and now and to begin to sense the massive, wonderful, yet tragic world education inhabits. Take a breath only for a moment though, for we have other educational worlds to travel through, intimated by scratched markings on the surface of a school desk, even a desk as spectacularly plain as the trapezoid one above. If it has been around for long enough in a school, we would notice something transformative on its surface, something that revealed the force of living beings using its material reality on a daily basis.

For sitting on the chair, at a desk, in classrooms of all the schools in the world are human beings; and what curious creatures they are. So we jump from the collective materiality of schooling to the student sitting at a desk, with the view of exploring their individual material functioning (figure 2.12).

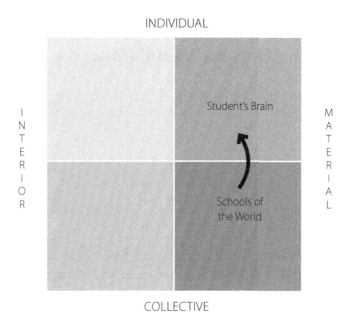

Figure 2.12 Shifting from the material/collective to the material/individual

Chapter 3

How the 'brain' learns

At an atomic level we would not be able to see any difference between what is going on in the materiality of a school desk and the materiality of a schoolchild sitting at the desk. Both would show a buzzing world of electrons, protons, mesons, and so on. If we expanded our level of focus outwards, at what point would a distinctly educational reality emerge? We could say, with some certainty, that the materiality of schooling coalesces out of atomic soup with desks, chairs, windows, books, writing equipment and all the other elementary artefacts of the classroom. With the physical body of a student, the smallest material unit of analysis would be something very different, something like a neuron interacting with other neurons in a specific way. At a microscopic level, a neuronal network is an alive process, humming with charges and changes; completely different from the dead micro-fibres of a piece of paper overlapping each other to give a surface. Neurons actively change their state and connections when learning happens; paper fibres absorb and break when written upon, they do not dynamically adapt and change themselves in an organised way. Note that the educational imagination is jumping from a tight focus on the smallest unit of analysis in the material dimension of the physical school to the smallest unit of analysis in the material dimension of the physical body of a learner. On the one hand it is the smallest of moves, from a material desk to the materiality of a learner occupying the desk. But on the other hand it is a massive jump from something that is not alive to something that is alive; and more than just alive: something that is self-aware.

It is important, at this point, not to lose our focus on education by suddenly plunging into the intricacies of neuroscience and biology. Our question is not about how the human body and brain function, but what the assorted smallest and largest structures are in the field of education; and the smallest physical unit of learning in us is something like a neuron interacting with other neurons in a specific way. I use the word specific because we are not looking at how the brain functions in general, or how neurons function specifically, but what happens to students when involved in school learning. We have to be clear that the interaction we study is an educational reality, not just brain activity. This book is not about neuroscience. It is about education in all its heights and depths, which touches, at its finest level of focus, on the way neuronal functioning helps us understand the process of learning; not just any learning that happens as life teaches us its hard and beautiful lessons, but the way we learn within educational frameworks. There are a growing number of texts that combine neurobiology with education. One that I have found particularly useful in getting this focus right is *The Unified Learning Model: How Motivational, Cognitive and Neurobiological Sciences Inform Best Teaching Practices* by Shell et al. (2010). I have used it to structure the first third of this chapter.

Episodic and semantic knowledge

We can start our search for what is distinctly educational in the brain by looking for a distinction similar to one between everyday experience and formal school knowledge. Such a distinction can be found in the difference between episodic knowledge and semantic knowledge. Episodic knowledge develops in the process of living our life and is immersed in the tastes, smells, feelings and details of particular daily experiences. We don't normally have to force ourselves to attend to these experiences: they happen and we are in the happening, participating in its situated richness. The episodic nature of this knowledge results in specific detail fading quickly from long-term memory while habits and dispositions grow from the repeated nature of daily events surrounding eating, playing and sleeping.

For example, allow me to ask you how you spent your evening precisely 30 days ago. The evening will not spring readily to mind. You could do some heavy reconstructive work to get there, by trying to track something specific that happened on that day, or the previous day, and work from the memory outwards, but as time periods get longer and longer you land up with trends: Thursday night is burger night, Friday night is getting out night and Sunday night is for romance, or should have been if we weren't both so bloody tired. It's the repeated harmonies in the ebb and flow of ordinary life that combine into scripts that govern how we conduct ourselves; into long-term memories of what our bedroom looked like; and into routines that allow us to function automatically and do things without paying much attention to them. The massive experiential richness of the actual event dwindles into the comfortable trace of the usual.

Semantic knowledge is memory that is specifically not about our own life: it does not come automatically and easily from the personal process of experiencing life (Shell et al., 2010, p. 38). It has a context, although this is not the rich intimacy of our own lived context, but one that has to be built up, step by painful step. Although semantic knowledge starts flush in the thick of lived experience, it has to construct a context that is delocalised, one that specifically relates to the knowledge event rather than to our own lives. Semantic knowledge will always be located within an episodic context as we are always learning in our bodies here and now, but it will slowly separate off from the lived context towards its own specific contextual set. That is why it is really important to ensure the lived experience of learning at school is a positive one because semantic knowledge starts out in the episodic experience of that classroom on that day and resonates with previous experiences and events. But as semantic knowledge grows it has to separate itself from the particular experience of everyday life and develop the internal logic of what is being actively learnt in its own terms.[19] It formalises itself.

The key image to hold in mind when thinking about the difference between episodic and semantic knowledge is that episodic knowledge starts off rich and full of the tastes, sounds, touches, sights and feelings of life and reduces itself to a routine script of what is common to all the variations; whereas semantic knowledge starts off small and impoverished and slowly grows, link by artificial link. When a child starts to learn how to read you can see this fruitful tension at its clearest. On the one hand the teacher will labour to keep an experiential episodic richness and play in the classroom whilst at the same time beginning to introduce the completely arbitrary logic of letters and their combinations. Slowly, but surely, the child begins to learn explicitly something that builds on itself and creates formal links with concepts that are higher than it, or examples that are different from it, creating an organised semantic web (figure 3.1).

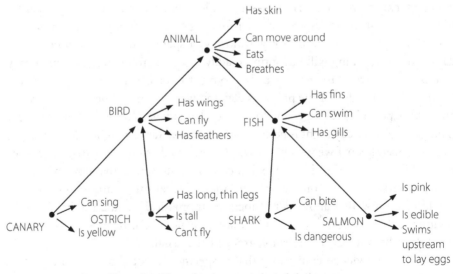

Figure 3.1 Hierarchical semantic knowledge structure

Note how this resonates with the educational imagination travelling up to more abstract concepts (canary – bird – animal) and across to equivalent levels (bird/ fish; canary/ostrich/shark/salmon). But also note that a child who has had a rich episodic set of experiences with canaries, ostriches, sharks and salmon will make far more sense of the formal structure. The episodic experiences, even though they have reduced to traces, provide a fertile soil. It's not an either/or with episodic and semantic knowledge; it's and/and. The key point I want to make, however, is that semantic memory needs directed attention and motivation for a sustained period. It does not come automatically as a part of living, eating, exploring your surroundings and sleeping. It is hard work no matter how well integrated into tastes, sounds and actions; hard work because we have to direct and hold attention on something that is arbitrary and formal, and because, as we all know, attention is limited.

Neuron basics

And it is the way neurons work when we pay attention that gets us closer to our educational unit of analysis rather than the intricate biology of the neuron in its own terms. It's how neurons function when we learn that is the focus, not its internal mechanisms; but even so we need a bare minimum of mechanical detail.

A neuron has two ends, one that receives impulses (dendrite) and another that releases impulses (axon). To release an impulse the neuron has to receive impulses that push it beyond its threshold. Only when this limit is broached does the neuron fire. In other words, the neuron gets excited from all the impulses coming its way. At a certain liminal point, if all these impulses sweetly hit the same spot, the neuron just can't help itself and has to fire away. I can relate. Unlike me, the more a neuron fires, the easier it is for it to fire again. The firing ability of a neuron changes through use. But it's not only that the firing threshold drops with use: the connections with other neurons involved in stimulating or receiving the firing are strengthened as well. If you are connected together and fire together then the connections are strengthened and it's easier to do it all again next time round. This gets us to a simple elementary definition of learning: 'Learning occurs when the firing ability of a neuron is changed' (Shell et al., 2010, p. 8).

The vital role of working memory

The problem is that there is an enormous amount of sensory stimulation pouring into us and circulating around us at any given moment and we can only attend to some of what is entering and circulating. The space where this happens is working memory and it is here that we hit the interconnection between learning and the functioning of our brain head on. If we had unlimited amounts of working memory and could pay attention to everything at once then learning would be something very different from that of human experience. The memory span of young adults when pushed to its maximum is around seven items, as discovered by Miller (1956) in his famous paper 'The magical number seven, plus or minus two'. We know this from the way we struggle to remember someone's cell phone number unless it has a sweet pattern.

However, most of our learning tasks do not involve simple bits, but deciding what to do with a bit: is it right or wrong, up or down, inside or outside, here or there? Notice that this means we shall remember a lot less than seven items because our working memory has some of its space taken up with decision-making processes. This has resulted in differences between popular accounts of the capacity of working memory, varying all the way from 7 plus or minus 2 items to one item on which a decision is being made. The more complex the decision to be made, the more working memory is taken up with the options presented by the decision. More recent research points to four slots of working memory being more likely than 7 plus or minus 2, but the point holds – the more complex the action, the less bits you can work with.

It is the constricted way that working memory functions which fundamentally structures the learning process of the human species. The massive number of firing connections swim desperately to a restricting attention channel they have to flow through to get into long-term memory on the other side. Only some make it, but when they do we have the fertile production of knowledge. So what is this cervix of the brain called working memory and how does it work?

First, not everything you experience gets into working memory. There is way too much going on around and inside you to be dealt with by four slots. Your biological and cognitive make-up tends to allow what is novel or conspicuous into working memory. Second, if all slots of your working memory are taken up with a process, then other things, especially if they are not novel or conspicuous, are just ignored. This means that we are not really paying much attention to most of what is going on in our environment, as is shown by all sorts of experiments designed to make most of us look like idiots. One of the most famous is the passing a basketball video designed by Daniel Simons (you can try it yourself. Spoiler alert: if you want the video to work its magic, then don't read what follows until you try it.)[20]

The instruction you are asked to follow is to 'count how many times the players wearing white pass the basketball'. You then see six students, three in white and three in black passing two basketballs to each other. I concentrated hard on counting the passes and got it wrong, somehow counting sixteen instead of fifteen. What I did not see was a gorilla walk right into the middle of the group, beat his chest and then walk out. My working memory was taken up by counting the white players passing and trying to ignore the black players, so I ignored the black gorilla strolling in and out of the scene, because he moved at the same pace as the others and was also dressed in black.

My students experience something similar on teaching practice when I chat to them afterwards about their lessons. They were so busy trying to remember what they needed to say and do that they show a remarkable lack of awareness about what the students were doing. When I ask them afterwards about key events in the class, they have hardly any memory of them.

We all function partly like this: to concentrate on something, we withdraw our attention from other things. When I am concentrating hard I do not hear what is going on around me. My mother used to have to come right up to me and shout to break my concentration when I was listening to Jet Jungle and Squad Cars on the radio; and even then I experienced her voice as coming from a distance. What I concentrated on I tended to remember, especially if I thought about it afterwards. It's obvious on one level: learning requires attention on the one hand and repetition on the other. To do this properly you need to focus on the object at hand for a sustained period of time and then go over it again in some way. Attention is what keeps something in working memory from slipping away after twenty or so seconds; and repetition is what enables transfer from temporary memory to long-term memory. We have to be careful with repetition, as some pedagogues could read its importance as meaning rote learning and drill. Two points need to be made here: first, a distinction between shallow learning and rote learning; and, second, the need to transform what is being repeated for it to stick in long-term memory, especially with more complex areas of knowledge.

We cannot avoid shallow learning: it's a natural part of learning something new where initially you don't tend to get the full picture, or understand how the different parts hang together and the intricate nuances. But by sticking to the task, long-term memory develops out of a learner paying attention and making meaning. Rote learning is devoid of meaning: all that is focused on is getting the form of things into the mind through drilling. Just because you initially learn in a shallow way does not mean that you need to be drilled with rote memorising strategies.

You do need to repeat and go over what you are learning to embed it in long-term memory, but the repetition does not have to be in exactly the same form each time. Exactly the opposite, actually: it's in making meaning of the element – of coming back to it from different angles and placing it within larger networks that give it a frame – that a shift from temporary to long-term memory happens. As a temporary memory shifts into long-term memory it transforms; and the reason why it changes is that it has to be inserted into already existing networks in long-term memory. You don't just plonk something in long-term memory: it gets there in a more sustained and memorable way when you first get its essential meaning and second link it to other things you already know and understand. Getting the essential meaning and placing it in a larger network are really part and parcel of the same activity – making sense of something – because it is in seeing how the particular elements relate to other elements that the attachment of meaning happens. This means that the temporary memory has to be transformed into something that makes sense through connecting it to a relevant network. The larger and more dense the already existing set of connections, the more able you are to place an element in a bigger picture and see how it holds there, enabling its shift into long-term memory. As the gospel of Matthew notes, 'Whoever has will be given more, and he will have an abundance. Whoever does not have, even what he has will be taken from him' (Matthew 13:12, *New International Version of the Bible*).

The real danger of pointing at automatisation is that teachers think the take home pedagogic message is that drilling their pupils is key. The problem with drilling is that students lose focus and motivation, and if they are not actually attending to the task at hand when learning then its effectiveness is lost. You need to attend to the topic and the best way to work with attention is to make the topic interesting, worthwhile and relevant, not necessarily to everyday experiences, but to the growing semantic network of knowledge in long-term memory. And the more the student actually knows how to do this herself, the more she gets control of hir own meta-cognitive processes, then the more effective learning becomes. There are many reasons why we celebrate the independent learner who takes control of her own learning, but what we don't often see is that active learners (rather than drilled learners) are supported by the working of our brains.

The many become one and are increased by one: the wonderful world of chunking

What is interesting about connecting things into networks is that the element now holds as a moment in a bigger picture. If you understand the big picture, then you have the elements of the picture contained within it. This is a vital point regarding the intersection of pedagogy with the four slots of working memory, probably the most important point of this chapter. Why?

The reason is that the big picture with all its elements holds as one thing, needing only one slot of working memory. It is really hard, almost impossible, to increase the number of slots you have in working memory. It is far easier to develop your understanding of the connections between elements and build them up into a bigger pattern that holds, and become acquainted with how the pattern works, until a point is reached where the whole pattern is one functioning unit. This is what experts do. They don't have more slots in their working memory than novices: it's partly that they work with bigger chunks and this makes it look as if they have really quick, sharp minds. There is a classic test that reveals this involving chess grandmasters, A-level (mid-range) players, and novices (De Groot, 1965). Each set of characters were given two to ten seconds to memorise a chessboard position with 25 pieces. Grandmasters were astounding, recreating positions from scratch with 93% accuracy. That's basically getting only two of twenty-five pieces in the wrong place. A-level players were able to get approximately half the pieces in the right place and novices only a third. It would seem that grandmasters have photographic memories. I say 'seem' because if you take the same 25 chess pieces and put them randomly on the chessboard, then suddenly the grandmaster's memory is only as good as the novice next to him. He was not remembering 25 individual pieces and their places; he was remembering patterns of pieces (Chase and Simon, 1973). The thousands of hours spent playing and studying chess meant that the grandmaster was not playing with individual pieces, but with patterns of pieces, and patterns of patterns, each of which holds as one chunk.

You can see this if you watch the grandmaster closely as he reconstructs the board from memory (figure 3.2). First, he thinks a little and then places around six pieces down quickly. Then he thinks again before placing around another six down, and so on with the third and fourth sets. The setting down of the pieces occurs in bursts of patterns, not of individual pieces. The novice works with individual pieces rather than with patterns and so is really limited in this task.

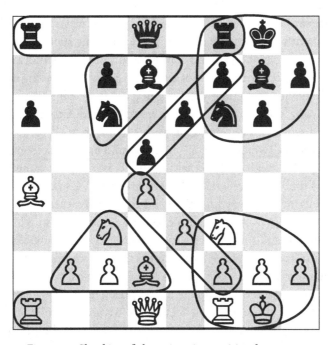

Figure 3.2 Chunking of chess pieces into positional patterns

I experienced this at first hand when playing a visiting chess grandmaster at my school, only he did not just play against me but against 29 other students as well, all of us arranged in a circle of desks in the hall. He walked from board to board taking a couple of seconds before making a move, with me, the novice, agonising about what move to make. I was working with individual pieces and trying to think ahead with something like the following thought process: if I move this piece here, then he can move this piece or this piece or this piece, which means I could then either move this piece or that piece, which means ... where was I again? And then he was back at my table, taking a couple more seconds before moving decisively. It was like a vice slowly strangling me: my options became more and more limited, I became pinned down and exchanges of pieces resulted in the loss of more of mine. Then, after going around the tables and playing with 29 other players, he came to my table, looked at the positions, made one move and it was checkmate. It felt like I was playing against a god, some kind of superhuman being. What I was really playing against was a person who had put many of the patterns and moves into long-term memory and was able to recall and manipulate them in working memory. As for me, I had no long-term memory network around chess, except how the pieces worked and two opening moves. I had to rely on working memory for individual moves, not for overarching patterns, and what I held in my head thirty seconds before just melted away.

The implications of this point for teaching and learning are clear, as numerous educators have pointed out (Kirschner, Sweller and Clark, 2006). I would like to put one implication forward in two complementary ways: the need for novice learners faced with novel information to have explicit instruction; and recognition of how crucial it is to build up dense complexes of integrated information in long-term memory as a key component of developing problem solving skills.

If you are a novice on X, then you are going to need clear and explicit guidance on X so that your long-term memory networks around X consolidate. If you are left to try to discover what is going on at this point, then all you have to rely on is working memory (which fades all the time) and arbitrary resonances in long-term memory (that might not be that useful.) This is the fundamental insight of cognitive load theorists such as Sweller, Kirschner and Clark. A novice can work on problem solving for a very long time and come away learning hardly anything about the problem. A worked example, on the other hand, in which every step is explicitly shown and the answer clearly given, results in novices grasping the process because they only have to comprehend the process, not discover it. As working memory focuses on these essential relations rather than thrashing around, the relations are laid down in long-term memory, enabling students to think progressively (*sic*) on their feet when it comes to solving a problem as they have the resources in long-term memory to help. It then becomes crucial to move away from explicit worked examples to more open problem solving and discovery type questions, as you want the learners to work with their own long-term memories, not follow step-for-step what is on the page. It is the dense collection of integrated information and strategies stored in long-term memory that enable effective problem solving, not some generic problem solving course that is supposed to work across all sorts of different domains.

Studies have worked out how many patterned chunks grandmasters carry in their long-term memory, and it is around fifty thousand (Chase and Simon,

1973). That is astonishing. But you are carrying thousands of chunks as well; only they are not chess patterns but chunks of letters called words. There is much debate about how many words a well-educated person actually knows (D'Anna, Zechmeister and Hall, 1991, pp. 109–122). But the argument is that what we consider exceptional in a grandmaster is similar to what we all do with language. Shakespeare, by the way, knew 66 534 words, if statisticians like Efron and Thisted (1976) are to be believed. The point is that schooling is about developing such extended sets of chunks in subject specific semantic knowledge networks.

Two key features stand out from the above discussion. First, to shift something from short-term to long-term memory it is important to place the item into an existing network and this means transforming the item so that it fits within it. The denser and more developed the network, the easier it is to locate the item in some part of it. Second, to increase working memory capacity it is almost impossible to increase the number of its slots, so the best route forward is to increase the size of the chunks. Notice that these two features are intimately related. Increased networks allow for improved transfer of an element into long-term memory and increased networks result in chunking, where what is worked with is not a single element but patterns of elements in a network. It is a virtuous circle, especially when these long-term memories are accessible to working memory.

Let's now go back to the previous discussion around episodic and semantic knowledge because the distinction between them is the difference between two kinds of ways networks can function. Episodic knowledge comes easily from the personal process of experiencing life. Semantic knowledge is built up, step by painful step, chunk by chunk, from elements that have a specific set of meanings and relationships that are not based on the stream of life, but on logical and defined associations. The larger and denser this defined network of relations, the more readily a semantic element finds a place in the network as a transformed part or moment of the network. This is because working memory looks for patterns in long-term memory similar to the element on which it is focusing. It's the foundational act of intelligence: to predict what is going to happen based on what has gone before. We all do this with episodic knowledge. Based on our experiences of the world, we predict what will happen based on past similar experiences. That is why we respect and listen to people with life experience as they are able to negotiate current occurrences intelligently based on a wealth of past associations.

The issue for education is how we do this for semantic forms of knowledge as well as for episodic knowledge. The more these semantic elements are built up into meaningful chunks, and the chunks organised into dense patterns or schema, the more working memory is able to cope with larger loads in quicker ways. Crucially, working memory is also able to find matches in long-term memory for what it is temporarily holding. The pedagogic struggle is to shift the matches from purely episodic similarities to matches that have both semantically dense and episodically rich resonances. A student needs to build up systematic networks of knowledge that allow for informed placement and chunking. This takes work. Unlike episodic knowledge that comes from experiencing life, semantic knowledge has to be built up through an artificial process that has non-local logics that shift away from processes of everyday existence. But once semantic knowledge networks build in long-term memory, an expansion of working memory capacity results, not only in terms of its ability to carry larger chunks, but also, with repetition, of its ability to work with increasing speed because it has access and assistance from long-term memory. And that means that more stuff gets into long-term memory more quickly; resulting in a further expansion of both working and long-term memory, and so on, in a virtuous cycle.

What this makes clear is that a non-negotiable goal of school learning should be an expansion of long-term memory, especially of the semantic knowledge type. Each time a chunk is retrieved from long-term memory, the knot of neurons at the base of the memory fire. If you are working with an extended complex semantic network in long-term memory, then you are activating massive parts of the network each time you retrieve an element of it. Crucially, each time the knot of neurons fire, the easier it becomes to fire the next time round. Simply put, the more you repeat something and the more you retrieve it from long-term memory, the quicker and easier the access to that memory next time round, and the less strain you put on working memory. And the more these memories are chunked, then the larger the meaning base that is activated.

Automatisation

Continuous practice eventually results in automatisation and although it is unclear how the neuronal base of this works, it is clear that automaticity frees up working memory for other activities. When an action or practice becomes automatic, what has happened is that all the possible wrong ways of doing something have been ironed out, and what is left is the successful groove with a limited set of actions that are well oiled. This makes the activity easier and faster. This easy speeding up is accentuated by the fact that neuronal firing speeds increase with continued repetition, resulting in very quick reaction times. When this is combined with the ability of your mind to focus on other issues that demand attention, you can attend to a complex problem space with more intelligence and openness. Earlier, I used the example of student teachers struggling to attend to everything happening in their classes because they were focused either on getting the information of the lesson correct, or control of the class. Either classroom control or the content of the lesson suffer, often both. An expert teacher, on the other hand, is able to teach the lesson and attend to all the emotional and managerial issues at the same time because much of what she is doing has become automatic, freeing working memory to attend to the many complexities of the classroom dynamic. As an aside for teacher educators, this means we should have different definitions of excellence for a novice and an expert. Excellence for a student teacher should not be defined in terms of what an expert teacher does, but on what a novice teacher can do well, given the fact that she is a novice.

From neuroscience to education

So if we start with a single neuron firing, and expand outwards towards what in this neuronal story resonates with the educational process, then we find it lies in the relationship of working memory to long-term memory, with a specific focus on the intersection with increasing growth of semantic knowledge and its dynamic interaction with episodic knowledge. Notice that we have moved away from the intricacies of the molecular functioning of the brain to more general functions of the mind (like working and long-term memory) and its intersection with knowledge types that are very hard to see in any meaningful way in the chemical reactions of the brain. The more we dig into the micro-architecture of the brain, the less relevant the application to education.

This is a key lesson for the educational imagination: how to negotiate the boundary where education ends and other worlds take over. It's an exceptionally hard judgement to make and the crossover line is blurred, with networks running outwards and inwards and across the line. A rule of thumb is always to hold in mind a pedagogic act and ask if what is being stretched towards still has educational relevance. Allow me to try to demonstrate this with the borderland between neuroscience and cognitive science.

Neuroscience is about neurons and how they function. Cognitive science is a more interdisciplinary focus on how minds work. We have to be really careful about how we apply neuroscience to education (Willingham, 2009). Education has a set of foci and goals that are very different from neuroscience. We focus on learning, a complex space involving a learner, teacher, knowledge forms and pedagogic processes with goals of character development, social and cultural activity, economic improvement and political engagement that spin outwards and upwards, as this book shows. Neuroscience focuses on neurons in the brain in a descriptive and analytic way. We can use this as educators, but only with care. Cognitive science has clearer applications to education because its focus is on how the mind/brain works, although we would immediately add that the learner is more than a mind and the learning process is more than about cognition. Closer to education would be cognitive psychology with its focus on perception, memory, language and mental representation; and even closer still would be developmental psychology with its focus on how humans develop over their life span. Closest to education would be educational psychology, until we get to pure education, whatever that is. Is there a way we can get these different levels clear to assist us in negotiating a space that goes from the smallest element of neuronal activity upwards to brain to mind to person to learning how to live productively in our modern world?

From neuron to human

The problem is that we are not simply working with levels of scale or complexity, but with jumps across ontological and functional categories, like brain and mind, individual and society; jumps in focus from neuronal interactions to learning processes; and jumps across different disciplinary fields with different types of research. If we simply take a scale approach that moves from smallest to largest, then we go from a synapse to an individual neuron, to a neuronal network, to a cortical sub-region, to the brain, to the central nervous system, to the body.

This zooming in and out of the body does important things. It gets us out of a tendency to think that we are really just our brains and the rest of our bodies are mere containers for its precious processes. Where it does not help is in the jump from the functioning of the material brain to the way our minds work, as this is a jump not in scale but in ontological type. Nor does it help us jump from a singular focus on the brain to the applied field of teaching and learning. The danger of developing an educational imagination stretching all over the show is that one refuses to discriminate between the radically differing realities lying very close to each other in the actual processes of teaching and learning. An educational imagination has to learn how to recognise and negotiate boundaries, not just indiscriminately jump around between them. Obviously all these levels and layers intersect and play out together, so it is often hard and hazardous to separate them out, but with practice and informed study, both the separation out of levels and their intersection become easier to see.

Neural and behavioural levels of analysis

One way to help imagine the connections between levels at this specific point is to separate a neural level of analysis from a behavioural level of analysis and show how they relate. Willingham and Lloyd (2007, p. 141) provide us with a useful diagram (figure 3.3) that does just this.

This chapter's point of focus is at the level of a cognitive construct – specifically that of working memory and long-term memory – for it is here, we have argued, that the smallest useful unit of analysis for educational purposes can be found. Note that a cognitive construct is not a neural construct. It uses much of the information about neural levels of analysis work, but it has shifted ontological levels to focus on mind rather than electrified meat. When we have gone into lower levels of analysis (like how neurons and neural networks function), this has been simply to give a grounding picture of working and long-term memory. Our major point of interest has been how working and long-term memory intersect with semantic knowledge and how this plays out in educational terms. This is a behavioural level of analysis located between cognitive and educational constructs. We have been careful not to focus on the millions of neuronal synapses between neurons or on our internal representations of the physical, social and personal world going on in our minds. This is too fine-grained a level of analysis for the educational imagination, not because it is invalid in its own terms, but because it sits outside the education boundary. One of the failures of the educational imagination is to pretend that it is allowed to go wherever it wants, because it is the imagination. All this results in is dilettantism and misapplication. There is a rigour to the educational imagination that comes from a defining of boundaries that gives it the limitations from which creativity can deepen and play. So at this point we are focusing on cognitive constructs in the mind, as these are the building block units of educational constructs that we will get to later in this chapter (such as cognitive load theory, reading theory or multiple intelligence pedagogy.)

NEURAL LEVEL OF ANALYSIS	BEHAVORIAL LEVEL OF ANALYSIS
	School
	Classroom
Central nervous system	Individual mind
	Educational construct
	Cognitive construct
Gross anatomic structure	
Nucleus, cortical subregion	
Neural network	Internal representation or process
Individual neuron	
Synapse	

Figure 3.3 Neural and behavioural levels of analysis

From molecular neuroscience to educational psychology

Kalra and O'Keefe (2011) attempt to illuminate these levels in a different way by contrasting how textbooks in educational psychology, developmental psychology, cognitive psychology, cognitive neuroscience and molecular neuroscience work differently, and it is fascinating to see how distinctive they are. Let's take the extremes of educational psychology (closest to education) and molecular neuroscience (furthest from education) and compare their overall perspective, research methods and specific focus.

The overall perspective of educational psychology is on the application of psychology to education for teachers; its research methods involve qualitative and quantitative methods about how children think and learn; and its focus is on how effective this research is to inform pedagogic techniques and curriculum construction.

The overall perspective of molecular neuroscience is intensely focused on how synapses function. Its research methods involve single cell recording, genetic manipulation and experiments with the impact on the synapse of assorted drugs;

and its focus is to work out the distinctive properties of neurons in relation to other cell types.

There is no doubt that molecular neuroscience has implications for education, but a massive amount of reworking is needed before any sense can be made of the highly technical research. As educators, we have to rely on the recontextualisation of molecular neuroscience to education that takes into account the massive difference in overall perspective, research methods and focus.

There is a danger in assuming that because molecular neuroscience has the smallest and most tangible focus area that it is possible to make educational recommendations based on its findings. There are some areas where this is the case, like dyslexia, where neurological disorders affect learning (Willingham and Lloyd, 2007), but for the most part molecular neuroscience is too fine-grained a level of analysis. This becomes obvious when we compare the different disciplinary research methods.

It should be clear that single cell recording of non-human animal studies does not have much to say about the pedagogy best suited to children studying science at grade 6 level in a context of poverty. It's as crazy as nuclear physicists waxing lyrical about the basis of our ethical and moral positions drawing on the functioning of the sub-atomic. That said, this should not stop the project to combine mind, brain and education into an interdisciplinary region that asks how research at the level of the mind and brain can inform educational policy and practice. It is just that the enormous difficulty of working between these levels has to be clearly seen and negotiated. We have started the process by using working memory and long-term memory as a focus point, as it gives us core cognitive constructs that exist at the intersection of cognitive neuroscience and cognitive psychology with powerful implications for teaching and learning, as seen in the Unified Learning Model of Shell et al. (2010) and the work of cognitive load theorists such as Sweller and van Merriënboer. It is in their work that you can find clear and precise accounts of how cognitive science intersects with pedagogy and instructional design.

Cognitive load theory

The stepping-off point for the intersection of pedagogy and our cognitive architecture is the simple point that our working memory is limited. If we are just remembering stuff, then we can hold around seven bits in our minds. But as soon as we start to process information through making sense of it by contrasting it, placing it and comparing it to what we already know, then we can only hold around two or three bits at the same time. Crucially, this information only stays in our working memories for around twenty seconds. Pedagogic practices have to take the limitations of working memory very seriously, for this provides the gateway to deep learning: every piece of knowledge has to pass through its gates, gates that have a limited carrying and holding capacity.

A curious feature of working memory is that it has two different channels that receive information, visual and auditory, and when both channels are used together, the capacity of working memory increases (Paivio, 1986, p. 86). If you listen to your teacher while at the same time seeing a demonstration on the board, you will understand more than when focusing on either on its own. I can testify to this effect from my own mathematical studies in the Khan Academy. Salman Khan has made around 4 000 videos that he has uploaded onto the Internet for students to learn maths from addition and subtraction all the way through to calculus. If you watch a video you will not see him talking, but will see the maths problems being written out. You listen to him talking while seeing the problem unfold.

This simple method, used by teachers across the world, makes maths easier to understand than simply working from the textbook or listening to an explanation. Videos that actually film a lecturer talking waste your working memory capacity. You don't need to see someone talking; you need to hear him or her. But if at the same time as hearing them you watch examples, diagrams, figures and key phrases, then your capacity to understand and remember increases. This dual coding of information is also what makes power point presentations that simply put up what is being said boring. Your visual channel works at a different speed to your audio channel: as a result you read the slide in a couple of seconds and then have to sit through the laborious verbal account of exactly the same thing. Don't put up your words on power point; put up supporting images.

Take a look at figure 3.4, based on Cooper (1998), to catch what my words are describing.

Even if you are using both audio and visual channels to increase the capacity of working memory, it still has a very limited carrying capacity. Earlier in this chapter we saw how chunking provided the key technique to overcome this limitation. It might be that you can only carry around four elements at a time in your working memory, but the size of these chunks can vary from a single bit of information to a massive networked process. Suddenly, what seemed to be a terribly limited capacity can be expanded almost to infinity, not by increasing the number of slots in working memory, but by increasing the size and complexity of the chunk. It is the networked schemas you carry in your long-term memory that give your working memory real power. If you do not have these complex schemas in your long-term memory, then you are doomed to work with around four tiny elements at a time, rather than with four huge processes. You can see this in figure 3.4 with long-term memory. Either you work with the tiny elements at the bottom or with the massive chunks at the top that include the elements underneath them within their processes.

The pedagogic question then arises: how do we increase schema construction in long-term memory? It becomes pedagogically imperative to work on getting information into long-term memory in an organised, schematic, way.

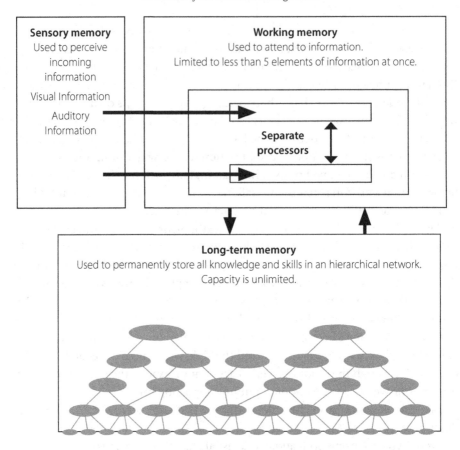

Figure 3.4 Flow diagram from sensory memory to working memory to long-term memory

But even if you have these complex schemas in your head, working memory can still be limited by having to pay attention to the way they work. With increased practice, many of the schemas start to function automatically. You don't have to think about it, it just comes spontaneously in habitual form. The more automated the process, the more working memory you will have to attend to the problem at hand. It's not only pedagogically imperative to build complex schemas, but also to automate them.

The place you build schemas is in working memory, so pedagogy must attend to the cognitive load expected of the student and ensure that working memory is not overwhelmed or starved. This is a tricky process because the more experienced the student is in the topic under exploration, the more developed hir schemas will be, meaning that more can be done, more quickly. If the student is a novice then care must be taken with the cognitive load as the carrying capacity of working memory will be limited. So, what pedagogic techniques can be used to reduce cognitive load by focusing on what is intrinsically necessary and eliminating elements that are extraneous? What can be cut away to make the load lighter, but still keep what is crucial for understanding, meaning making and the construction of schemas? Sweller, van Merriënboer and Paas (1998) identify six pedagogic techniques that reduce extraneous cognitive load for novices:

1. *Goal free effect*: Don't give the long-term goal of the problem under exploration at the same time as the problem itself. Rather focus on the problem and allow the goal to emerge once the problem has been understood (figure 3.5). If you reveal the goal before tackling the problem, then the students have to try to work out the relationship between the problem and the goal before they have understood the problem.

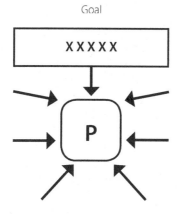

Figure 3.5 Goal free effect

2. *Worked example effect*: Don't just give novice students a problem to solve. Rather start with a worked example (figure 3.6) that shows the steps of the problem and how to solve it in its simplest form.

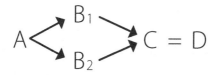

Figure 3.6 Worked example effect

3. *Completion problem effect*: Once the students have been given a worked example provide a problem that has some of the steps already learned and get them to complete it (figure 3.7). By reducing the size of the problem space to one or two steps that need completion you reduce extraneous load.

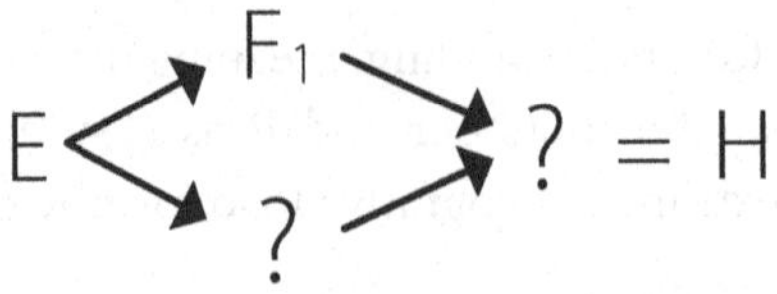

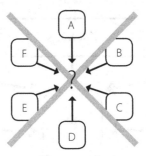

Figure 3.7 Completion problem effect

4. *Split attention effect*: Be careful of multiple sources of information that expect students to integrate the different bits (figure 3.8). Rather provide one integrated source of information on which they can focus.

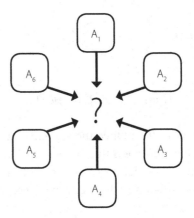

Figure 3.8 Split attention effect

5. *Modality effect*: If you are going to use different sources, then make sure that you combine auditory with visual channels. For example, replace a visual combination of a picture and a written explanation with a picture and an auditory explanation.
6. *Redundancy effect*: Be careful of multiple sources of information that all do something similar (figure 3.9). Rather have one source that does it all properly.

Figure 3.9 Redundancy effect

The key reason why you want to free up some space for working memory is that it needs space to make sense of the problem at hand, struggle with it and make meaning of it, so that the element of knowledge can be placed within an ever-growing schematic set developing in long-term memory. This process of meaning making also increases cognitive load, but it is a germane cognitive load that results in the crucial shifting of information from the limited world of working memory into knowledge networked within the infinite world of long-term memory. It is this germane cognitive load that must be increased by cutting away extraneous elements.

In effect, the total memory capacity we have inside ourselves when engaged in a task is taken up by three different kinds of load (figure 3.10): the intrinsic load of the task itself; the extraneous load of instructional choices around how to learn the task; and the germane load that comes with thinking about the task and making meaning from it (see http://kellymorganscience.com/why-designing-experiments-is-so-hard-for-students-what-we-can-do-to-help/).

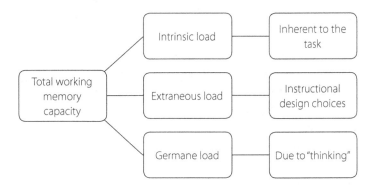

Figure 3.10 Total working memory capacity

For a person skilling herself in pedagogic imagination, this level of focus on working memory provides precise pedagogic variables that assist in both the descriptive analysis of learning and proscriptive advice about how to improve learning.

1. *Intrinsic load*: some tasks are more complex than others due to their inner make up and what they already expect the learner to be able to understand and do. Doing a calculus problem expects you already to have mastered algebra. If you do not have a good working knowledge of algebra, you will really struggle with a calculus problem even if it is carefully worked out for you. So one way to make the intrinsic load more manageable is to ensure that the basics needed to do the task are already well understood. A student with a working understanding of calculus will find a calculus problem easier than a novice calculus student.

2. *Extraneous load*: involves instructional strategies to teach and learn a task. You cannot avoid extraneous load, but you can reduce it by becoming skilled in those pedagogic choices that work to focus attention on the problem at hand, rather than distract attention with showy side effects. The six effects listed above provide a good beginner's guide. I say beginner because the six effects work best for novice learners of a task, not experts. Experts enjoy cracking a difficult, obscure, multiple task, but don't assume that because experts like it a novice will like it as well. In all likelihood, the novice will collapse with cognitive overload.

3. *Germane load*: the work done by thinking, reflecting and making meaning of a task. It is vital that space is left in working memory for this process otherwise the academic work done does not make it into the bigger schematic structures of long-term memory. Even worse, without meaning making, schematic structures in long-term memory stay thin and weak.

It is at this level of focus that the educational imagination can feel the powerful contribution cognitive science makes to pedagogy. We have not gone into ever-finer details about the chemical composition of the synapse, or the micro-architecture of the brain, important as these are. That is left for specialists in the neuro and cognitive sciences. What we have found in the work of cognitive load theory is a micro-level of focus that has direct pedagogic purchase. If we keep this combined focus on our cognitive architecture and its educational implications, but expand one level upwards towards a more general picture of the developing mind, what do we find?

A general model of the developing mind

A general model of the architecture of the developing mind would not be a picture of the brain, or a neural map of brain functioning, as it would need to work with a variety of cognitive constructs in the mind and hold them together in a developmental system that speaks to education. Something like figure 3.11 illustrates how to do a model of the mind rather than a picture of the brain (Demetriou, Spanoudis and Mouyi, 2010).

What makes the model so elegant is the way it represents four different features of our minds in one diagram. The first is stages of development, represented as four different stages going upwards from sensorimotor to abstract (four stages of general development levels). The second is the core capacities that run as the spine through the model. We have partly dealt with this core in terms of working memory and shown how to increase the speed, span and control of core capacities through automaticity, chunking and motivated attention. The third feature is the specialised capacity spheres that point to the working of our minds with different aspects of existence in specially adapted ways.

Finally, we have the hyper-cognitive system that self-reflexively builds up a systematic set of schemas and models. It's a key process as it catches the way students take control of their own learning by observing what happens to them when they learn and then learning how they learn. It's partly what is developed when working with the germane load of a task. It gets students to take control of their own processes, make them meaningful and place them within bigger schemas. So we have a basic core; different domains of thought that arise from the various types of information, relations and problems we encounter in the world (specialised capacity spheres); different capacity spheres going through general development levels; and, finally, that part of our minds that self-reflexively makes sense of it all.

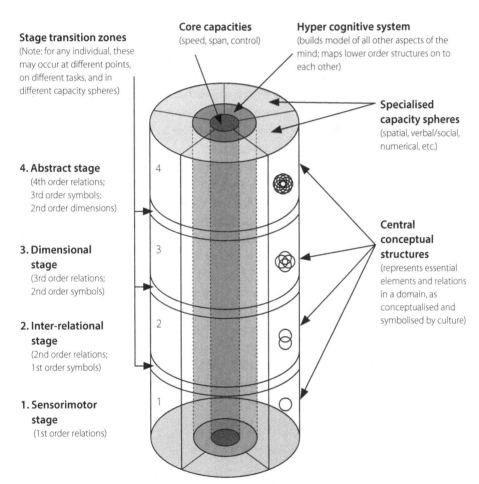

Figure 3.11 *General model of the architecture of the developing mind integrating concepts from Demetriou and Case*

The diagram is a prime example of a sophisticated educational imagination at work. It has shifted from a literal image of the brain to a combination of abstract elements held together in one image. But it does more than this as I hope to show in the following pages: it breaks specific limiting ways in which we have historically thought about human development and education. The first is to think that we go through general stages of development without taking into account that different specialised capacities develop at different speeds in different ways. The key breakaway point is to realise that we have different domains of thought that do different things, rather than just one overall path of development.

Domains of thought

A key operating principle of the education imagination is that it needs to move up and down all the levels that are educationally relevant. Once you get used to this climbing idea it becomes really important to grasp the different domains you need to master when climbing. For example, when climbing through levels of development in thinking, you have to recognise that there are different types of thinking, each of which needs its own climbing requirements. It's not only that the educational imagination must travel through levels; it has to understand the different domains it travels through as well.

There is some dispute about how many different domains of thought we have and how they relate to each other. But rather than get into a debate around how many, I would prefer to give a brief account of six of them and how they develop from elementary to more complex structures so that you can see how different domains work with similar levels. Each domain starts with an elementary way of dealing with specific aspects of the world and then develops over time into more complex ways.

Categorical reasoning
We all simplify the complexity of the world by predicting what will happen based on what we have already experienced. We expect similar events to produce similar outcomes and do this almost from birth. This domain gives us 'the seeds of inductive inference' (Demetriou, Spanoudis and Mouyi, 2010, p. 15) that build into understandings of similarities and differences between objects. These different objects are classified and ordered, giving us means to organise the complexity of the world in predictable ways.

Quantitative reasoning
The world is continually in a state of change. Things increase and decrease, break into parts or come together. From a very young age we have the ability to work with increase and decrease. As we get older this ability improves and we develop ways of counting, sharing, splitting up or keeping things for ourselves (Demetriou, Spanoudis and Mouyi, 2010, p. 15).

Spatial reasoning

The world has objects of different sizes and shapes that are near or far away from us. To negotiate this aspect of the world we develop ways to track their movement and mentally rotate what they look like (Demetriou, Spanoudis and Mouyi, 2010, p. 15). This helps us recognise objects from different angles and work between them.

Causal reasoning

When we push something it moves. Our basic interactions with the world show that we have an effect on the world: our cry produces a mother; a thrown object moves away from us. These basic experiences develop into a causal understanding of the world where we begin to experiment with what things work and what things don't, eventually developing systematic ways to isolate cause and effect relations.

Social reasoning

From a very young age we recognise human beings as different from other species and respond to smiles with a smile and a growl with a cry. This develops into an ability to work out what is going on inside other human beings based on their actions and appearance and to respond accordingly, eventually resulting in decentring, where we can take on the role of the other.

Verbal reasoning

Verbal reasoning to some extent works across the above domains as it enables social interaction, guides actions and combines insights from different domains into coherent inferences. Basic reasoning such as 'if this then that' and 'either this or that' develop an ability to work on relationships between things or processes and this develops into truth and validity relations where the honesty and reliability of the statements are evaluated.

Combining domains of thought with levels of development

Although these domains are separated off for ease of presentation, this in no way means that they do not intersect and overlap. The danger here is that once you grasp that there are different domains, you then imagine that they have to be separate. The best way to show how to get beyond a silo way of thinking is graphically. In figure 3.12 you can see that each domain is distinct, but there are places of connection (Rose and Fischer, 2009, p. 414).

Nor is it necessary that all the domains develop at equal times in equivalent ways. There are different developmental trajectories (figure 3.13) that can result in different levels of development at different times (Rose and Fischer, 2009, p. 416). Some domains do not necessarily become as highly developed as others.

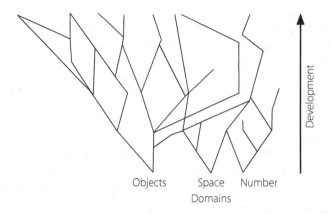

Objects Space Number

Domains

Figure 3.12 A developmental web for Piagetian domains of knowledge

Note that I am demonstrating this spreading and inter-related pattern of hierarchical development because it assists the educational imagination to discriminate between different domains or streams flowing through the same set of levels. This book is all about climbing through different kinds of levels. But even when one stays within one terrain – levels of intellectual development – it is possible to find that there are different streams running through the levels. This is a key discriminatory ability the educational imagination must master. And it must be able to imagine the different streams working at different speeds and in different ways, as can be seen in figure 3.13. To represent the same point using Demetriou's model we can show one domain reaching the fourth level and another only reaching the third (figure 3.14).

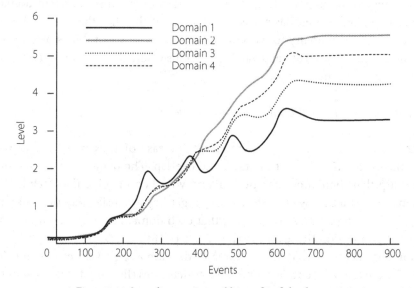

Figure 3.13 Spreading patterns of hierarchical development

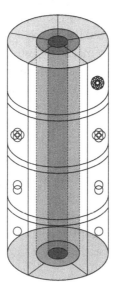

Figure 3.14 Spreading patterns of hierarchical development using the Case/Demetriou model

We can see in figures 3.13 and 3.14 a personal developmental trajectory that has different domains at different levels of development. This can be contrasted to another personal development trajectory (figure 3.15) that has managed to develop the different domains up to the same level (Rose and Fischer, 2009, p. 415).

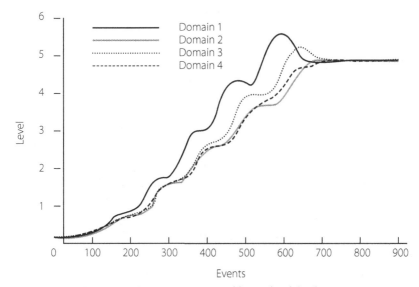

Figure 3.15 Converging pattern of hierarchical development

Figure 3.15 is crucial because it gets you to think back to a synthetic possibility of convergence once you have grasped the possibility of divergence. Just because the different domains diverge does not mean that one cannot get them to converge. Is it not worthy to aim at a balanced and harmonious set of domains as an educational ideal, rather than overdevelopment of some and underdevelopment of others?

Getting beyond simple and inaccurate models of the mind

What I like about the preceding five figures is how they challenge three overly simplified and restricting models of the way our minds work (which we will look at over the next three pages). Figures 3.11–3.15 enable the educational imagination to work in supple and lithe ways across levels of development and domains of thought, and shine a clarifying light on overly simple images of 'levels of development (3.16). IQ (3.17) and multiple intelligences (3.18).

Ladder of development

The first outdated model (figure 3.16) is a simple ladder of development based on the view that we go through set stages at set times.

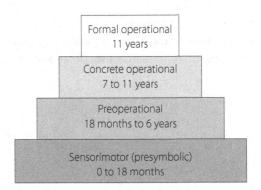

Figure 3.16 Basic stages of development based on Piaget

There is nothing wrong with initially learning about stages of development in this way. As climbers through an educational landscape we need to start with baby steps and the simplified view of Piaget's stages of development does teach us the basic rules of climbing.

But Piaget took us much further than this. He was a master of the climbing device and we have used his tools to climb even further. We don't simply have stages of development; we have different domains of thought developing at different rates to different levels. We also have the dawning recognition that if the domains have places of connection that work together, then it is risky to push for a speeding up of one domain at the expense of the others, for although separate they also inter-relate.

Finding the g-spot: intelligence quotient

The second out-dated model (figure 3.17) is one that assumes that behind all these different domains of thought is one general form of intelligence that can predict how we perform across all domains. This has been a blight on the educational landscape for over a century.

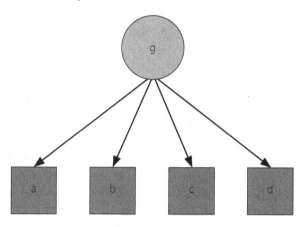

Figure 3.17 Single factor 'g' determines performance across domains 'a', 'b', 'c' and 'd'

This assumption is that no matter what the domain, a single factor determines performance across all domains; something called 'g' for general intelligence. If we did four very different types of tests (a,b,c,d) that worked with different domains we would tend to perform at the same level in each because general intelligence ability is at the heart of how we perform in all four tests.

Multiple intelligences

With the realisation that we have different domains of thought, it became clear that it was possible to perform differently in different tests depending on the domain and the test. But this recognition can result in a third oversimplified model suggesting that we have lots of different types of intelligence and nothing holding them together. In figure 3.18, there are six different types of intelligence, each measured by two different tests. For example, verbal intelligence (1) could be measured by a spelling test (a) and a grammar test (b): how well you do in the tests has everything to do with your verbal intelligence and not much to do with any other type of intelligence.

This is close to Gardner's multiple intelligence theory (MIT) view that has become so popular in schools across the world. At the intuitive heart of MIT lies a simple recognition that individuals can be strong certain skills but weak in others. Gardner formulated this position as a critique of the general intellectual potential view. Surely some individuals are better at some things than others and this cannot be condensed into one general number? Gardner

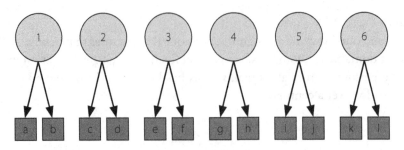

Figure 3.18 Separate factors determine performance in different domains

developed seven types of intelligence, recently updated to nine. This breaks open the educational imagination to the possibility of teaching in different ways for different intelligences. The problem with this position is that it does not accurately represent how the core capacities central to the functioning of our minds impact the different types of intelligence. To put it crudely, we have both a general intelligence function *and* multiple intelligences. If there are four tests (a, b, c and d as in figure 3.19) that work with two separate domains of thought (1 and 2), there are strong correlations both to specific domains of thought and to general intelligence (g). Willingham (2004) provides an excellent review of MIT and I have used his critique to format this discussion and the figures 3.17–3.19. I strongly recommend his blog found at www.danielwillingham.com.

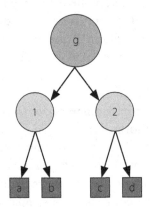

Figure 3.19 Combination of general intelligence (g) and different domains of
intelligence (1, 2) and tests for the domains (a, b, c, d)

General mental ability tends to predict how strong or weak performance will be in different domains of thought; and the domains of thought tend to predict performance in the two related tests in contrast to the other tests. Don't think that because you have broken away from a single restricting view of intelligence into multiple intelligences that you have successfully extended the educational imagination. It's only half the story. Take a look at how Demetriou depicts (figure

3.20) the hierarchical relationship between the six domains of thought and a more general mental ability (Demetriou, Spanoudis and Mouyi, 2010, p. 14). For our purposes the factor analysis is not important. Rather, it is the way the above analysis catches how the six domains stand as both separate and related to each other through a more general mental ability. It is as much a part of the educational imagination to work with convergence as well as divergence.

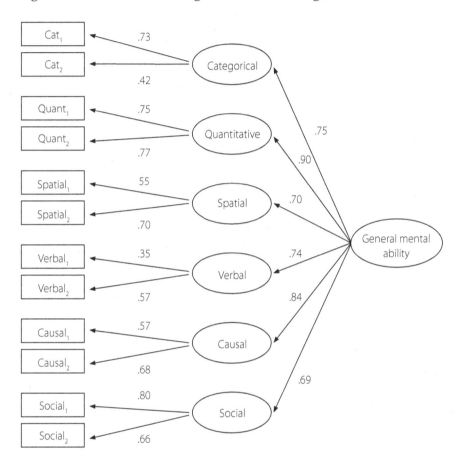

Figure 3.20 Hierarchical relationship between six domains of thought and more general mental ability

What gives Demetriou's model of the mind its synthetic elegance is how it shows all three out-dated models (basic stages, general intelligence and multiple intelligences) to have insightful elements, but to be severely limited on their own. The core capacities of speed, span and control refer to a general mental ability, but show how this core relates to more specific domains of thought that have their own functioning principles. The domains of thought catch Gardner's insight into multiple intelligences, but show how these also work with a central core; and the general development levels highlight how stages of development work, but relate this to different domains that can develop at different times and speeds. All of these factors have to take serious account of the hyper-cognitive system that gives us independence and control over our own intellectual functioning. Demetriou's model is a triumph of the educational imagination in terms of levels, domains, core functioning and the sweet wrapping of self- reflexivity.

To end off this chapter I would like to stay with the contrast between Gardner's multiple intelligences and Demetriou's model because it illustrates the seductiveness of thinking that diversity is the acme of imagination. The seduction runs something like this. The more intelligences we have the more creative possibilities for teaching and learning open out, demanding a pedagogy where we teach different children differently because of their unique combinations of multiple intelligences. Is that not the height of the educational imagination?

No, it is not, although when Howard Gardner's *Frames of Mind: The Theory of Multiple Intelligences* was published over thirty years ago in 1983 it did seem so. How is it, you might ask, that a theory pointing to a wide range of intelligences rather than one general Intelligence Quotient (IQ) could be bad for the educational imagination? Surely knowing that we are made up of different sorts of intelligences must be a good thing, educationally speaking? If each of us has a different intelligence profile just like our own unique fingerprint, and if understanding what this unique combination is gives a better ability to work out how to teach and learn, then we had better implement multiple intelligence pedagogies in all our classrooms as soon as possible. It should result in a massive improvement in learning as each student learns in a way best suited to her profile. Many teachers have had the personal experience of struggling to get a concept across in a particular fashion, and then, after shifting to a completely different way of doing it, finding their learners grasping it. There is no doubt that different ways of teaching a concept can have a radical impact on understanding and that some learners tend to grasp a concept better when using a particular type of representation. Teachers and researchers knew this long before multiple intelligences came along. The reason why learners start to understand the concept is not because it resonates with their particular type of intelligence profile, but because the concept has been better represented or because the multiple angle of view has increased understanding. The risk with teachers who use MIT to structure their lessons is that they might confuse the best ways to represent a topic with different intelligences of students (Willingham, 2004). And there lies the danger, for by trying to represent the concept in ways that best fit the intelligence profile of the student, the teacher can forget to represent the concept in ways that best fit the concept.

I was a history teacher in a past life and when covering the Anglo-Boer War, I used photographs, maps and diaries, not in an attempt to work with the different learning styles of my students, but to best represent the Anglo-Boer War. When doing Hitler I played some of his speeches, not to resonate with the auditory learning style of some of my learners, but because this presentation method best caught the hypnotic power of Hitler. I worked with different modalities in presenting my lessons, not because I was taking into account the different multiple intelligence profiles of my students, but because these were good ways to present the topic. There is far too little time in a classroom to waste it trying out different modalities of learning that are not really suited to the topic at hand, but resonate with the intelligence profile of the student. To get learners to construct letters out of twigs because they are kinaesthetically oriented is to waste time because we have excellent research on the best ways to teach letters to children. That is what is important; not that they spend half a day arranging twigs into patterns because it provides a feel for letters. Research on learning the alphabet does point to the importance of using different modalities, but this is based on systematic ways of getting all the children in the class to experience and make meaning of the letters, not on trying to accommodate different intelligence profiles. If you want to improve learning, then focus on what needs to be learned and how this can be done in deep and meaningful ways that bring out the essence of the concept.

What makes the adoption of MIT in classrooms even more worrying is the lack of empirical proof for separate multiple intelligences. We saw earlier in this chapter that recent work in neuroscience and cognitive development points to a general processing efficiency of the brain that carries through to different domains of intelligence (Demetriou, Spanoudis and Mouyi, 2010). If you have a really good working memory and can process information quickly and reflectively, this is going to carry through to the particular domain with which you are working, whether this be verbal, spatial, mathematical or social. There are different domains of intelligence, only they are not as separate as Gardner would have us believe. There is no solid empirical evidence for multiple intelligences in the form that Gardner has described.

It's not only empirical support for MIT that is lacking, but empirical support for its effectiveness in classrooms. It doesn't work that well as pedagogy. It complicates the lesson, over-individualises it, and makes feedback really difficult because so many different things are happening at the same time. It obscures the content of the lesson by making the manner of presentation dominate the concept. Multiple intelligence pedagogies do work sometimes, but this is mostly due to gifted teachers working in optimal conditions; the point here being that these kinds of teachers can make anything work.

Why, if MIT is both wrong as a theory of intelligence and ineffective as a pedagogic strategy, does it still carry so much power and conviction for teachers and parents? One reason could be that it gives us hope when struggling with calculus, grammar, Shakespeare, a science equation or anything really difficult. Maybe we can't get it because it's just not suited to our particular intelligence profile, that we have other intelligences. Everyone everywhere is intelligent in something. We just have to find what it is. We do have to find out what it is we do best, but this is a complex mix of intelligence, personality, environment, motivation and happenstance, not a simple finding of which intelligence profile we have from an ever-expanding list. The hard work is in squaring up to the task at hand with everything that you have and then persisting with it, not flipping around until you find what your own particular intelligence profile happens to be, after which everything will flow smoothly.

MIT gives us hope in the wrong place by attempting to improve student learning through trying to find just the right combination of factors for each student. It places the blame for poor performance on the lesson design being poorly adapted to the intelligence profile of the student; for if the design had been better adapted, then the student would have learnt, because the lesson would have inspirationally spoken to her own particular profile. Never mind that this is based on an over-simplified story of multiplicities of intelligences that results in over-complicated lesson design, over-stressed and fragmented teachers trying to do too many things, and learners who can blame their failure to learn on the inappropriateness of the lesson to their unique fingerprint. Never mind that MIT pedagogy results in a catastrophic increase in extraneous load. As parents and teachers we need to be far more careful about the fads pushing for admission into the precious sanctum of our classrooms.

That said, teachers across the world have resonated with MIT because it echoes something important in their own experiences. Different students learn differently and working out what these differences are has implications for teaching and learning. This is about learning styles, not multiple intelligences. Learning styles are different from multiple intelligences in that the former are closer to the reality of classroom life and the tangible practices of learning – how we concentrate, store, remember and make sense of knowledge. It looks at the practices of learning as a complex whole and explores the alternative ways different learners take through the process. For highly resourced schools with excellent and committed teachers, responding to a demanding parent body that insists their child gets individual attention, an explicit engagement with different learning styles is both rewarding and politically astute. But even here, with learning styles one has to be careful. Is it not better to induct learners into the rigours of the subject in its own terms, rather than bending the subject to the learning idiosyncrasies of a child? Will the child not learn more in the long run from engaging with what the subject demands rather than from what she demands of the subject? Humility is one of the key virtues of the educational imagination and at the heart of humility lies openness to the demands of the world, not what you demand of the world.

Let's stand back from this chapter and formulate where it has taken us. We started by trying to find the smallest functional element inside our material being that is strongly related to education. It is very tricky because unlike the materiality of a desk, the smallest functioning educational element inside us is part of a self-conscious and social animal. We started with a distinction between everyday experience and school knowledge and found a similar distinction within cognitive science between episodic and semantic knowledge. We then honed in on working memory as the key structure at a micro-level, tracking how knowledge is developed by getting through the astonishingly narrow and short-lived focus area of working memory into long-term memory. We showed how this basic functioning of our cognitive architecture has profound implications for teaching and learning; implications that have been best drawn out by cognitive load theory. We then broadened our focus to a more general model of the cognitive architecture of our developing minds and found it was vital to distinguish different specialised capacity spheres that operate as different streams or domains flowing at different speeds through developmental stages. We used this model to interrogate over-simplified models of development and the pedagogic dangers such over-simplifications hold, leading us finally into a critique of multiple intelligences. Just as chapter two went into the architecture of the school with its classrooms, desks and chairs, chapter three went into the architecture of our minds, looking for possible levels of movement up, down and across, always bearing in mind the instruction to stop when educational logics lose their purchase (figure 3.21).

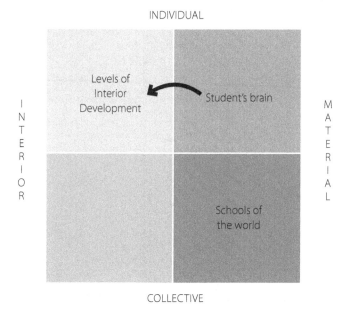

Figure 3.21 Shift from student brain to levels of interior development

If we review the book so far, we see that chapter 1 provided the widest angle possible by expanding outwards to all the schools of the world. Chapter 2 then narrowed the focus and honed in on the interior architecture, shifting from the school to the classroom, desks, chairs and writing equipment. We then jumped in chapter 3 from the desk to an individual learner sitting at the desk, but kept the narrow focus on the cognitive architecture of the learner's developing mind and brain. In chapter 4 we shift from more material accounts of the mind into its interior depths, with the question: how high can the mind reach as it learns? Just as we expanded schooling outwards from a specific location to districts, provinces, countries, continents and the world, so too we are going to expand the mind to ever higher levels, reaching ever greater levels of development. The mind enlarges within itself, encompassing more and more within its interior functioning. With schools we travelled across the world; with the mind we travel into the interior depths of expansiveness.

Chapter 4

Charting the space between demons and angels

There is something startlingly different between physical matter and the mind/emotion/will of a human being. Both exist as a part of the universe, but one is contained within an interiority that is self-aware. In the last chapter we explored the relationship between the functioning of a brain/mind and how we learn. In this chapter we turn to our interior being in its fullness. There is something extraordinary about the universe becoming mindful of its own existence, waking up to its own nature as it were, and this is what has happened with us. We are the universe becoming aware of itself, and, as far as we currently know, there are no other types of existence with such intense levels of self-awareness. We still tell ourselves that higher levels of awareness exist in our gods, but even here their instructions are normally quite clear – look within.

What do we find when turning from the materiality of existence towards its interiority? Another whole world springs into focus with very different organising patterns and principles. Stare into a desk and stare into a student's eyes. Something is the same – both exist. But something is different – the student stares back with an image of you in her. Over the last three chapters we have been working with the architecture of schools, classrooms and minds. Pens and tablets are on desks and chairs in classrooms in schools that are in school districts, provinces, countries, and continents in a world that is materially divided in racial, gender and spatial terms. Stare into a student's eyes and a different world opens up that is hard to see from the outside, even if this outside is the material functioning of the brain. We could perceive what was in a classroom by unpacking its contents on the field, but it's harder to unpack a learner's interior world onto the table, even with sophisticated brain scans. Our friendly alien, Tau, who has watched and wept over the tragic development of our material school world, would need a very different set of tools to work with the interior developments of an individual. How could Tau find a way to externalise this interior world so as to observe what was happening inside learners?

Opening the world inside a child – Piaget

The first person to conduct systematic, scientifically controlled experiments on the minds of children was Jean Piaget and because this was a controversial thing to do he used his own children. There was no need for ethical clearance. The only clearance he needed was from his wife, who helped him with the study, and as a result both of them played with their children for a substantial part of their childhood. For example, Piaget noticed that his seven-month-old daughter, Jacqueline, stopped playing with her plastic duck when she dropped it in a fold of a quilt and it disappeared from her view. Fascinated by her behaviour, he got the duck out, showed it to her, made sure she was interested in it, and then made it disappear again behind the quilt, at which point Jacqueline lost interest. Only at around ten months old did she begin to search for hidden objects. Could it be that, unlike adults, babies did not know things existed when not in their view? Could the baby be a solipsistic being, both unaware that she exists and unaware of any reality other than what is directly in front of her at the time? From a baby's perspective, maybe she is not born when emerging into the light of day from a long journey through a tight tunnel. Perhaps she only begins to realise she has a separate and lasting body that is different from the world over the first year of her life outside the womb: that there is an inside separate from an outside, that the inside is her, whatever that may be, and that the outside is not her, is different from her, but stays around even when she does not look at it.

It is an astonishing subject to stumble upon – the systematically different inner worlds of children and adults – and to chart in exquisite detail the developmental journey this inner world embarks on to reach maturity. Piaget is currently out of fashion, cartooned as a misguided biologist who experimented on individual children and thought they went through rigid stages of development that have now been disproved and supplanted by the work of Vygotsky. This is a caricature. Piaget published his first articles on snails in his middle teens; wrote a novel (*Recherché*) that chronicled his teenage angst and published it in the same year he got his doctorate, aged 22; chose humanities over the sciences; worked for the top psychologists of the previous generation and was fascinated by Freud and the unconscious; and was able to master multiple disciplines across the hard and soft sciences, continuing to do so for seventy years, meeting and engaging with many of the world's top thinkers and scientists in the process. Einstein, for example, was fascinated by Piaget's work, especially the problem of conservation of quantity.

Piaget loved to tell the story of Einstein grappling with the complexity of individual development, revealed in the example of conservation where 'you pour water into a glass of a certain shape, then into a glass of another shape, without changing the quantity. It was a delight for him [Einstein] to see what detours and complications you have to go through to prove the simplest bit of knowledge. He'd say, "It's a lot more complicated than physics!"' (Bringuier, 1980, p. 135). And it is more complicated: children stare back at you with curious energies in their eyes that are not reducible to $E=mc2$.

Piaget's initial focus was on cognitive development. Basically he found that as children get older they move through levels of cognitive development that continuously increase their range of possibilities (Bringuier, 1980, p. 137). Let's demonstrate this by asking you a simple question: what are the possible routes between points A and B below?

A   B

Ask a little child and she will give you a line

A ———————————————————————————————— B

Around the age of six the child will start to give you a small set of variations like straight, curved or zigzag lines.

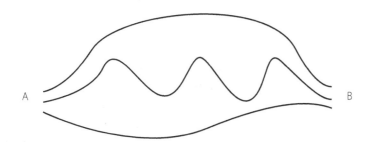

You, on the other hand, will find both solutions cute but obviously limited because there is an infinite number of routes from A to B, something you understand in an abstract way that is not about adding every single possible route together, but by logically understanding the principle. As a child moves through levels of cognitive development she becomes increasingly able to work systematically and abstractly with a given situation. Notice that there are two key elements at play here. First, there is the given situation that has a particular context and a particular set of possible responses (routes from A to B). Second, there are the procedures the child invents and experiments with to solve the given problem. At the heart of

Piaget is the meeting point between all the necessities a given situation contains and all the possible ways a child can intersect with these necessities until she reaches a point where her possible solutions closely match up to the necessities demanded by the situation. We tend to focus on the different levels of cognitive development, as you will find if you do a search for Piaget on the Internet. What Piaget was interested in was what drove the process through the levels. The more time he spent researching these processes of transformation the more he became fascinated by what he called reflective abstraction. Allow me a personal example.

When my daughter was in Grade 2 (end of 2012), she had no difficulties with addition and subtraction, and I really enjoyed helping her with homework. Then multiplication came along, and I struggled to explain how it worked. She could do her 1x table and her 10x table because there are simple rules behind it (repeat the same number or add a zero); and she kind of got the 2x table, because it simply involves doubling, but I could see she did not initially understand what multiplication really was or why it worked the way it did. When I did multiplication with zero she had no problems with numbers up to a hundred, but then suddenly insisted that 100x0 = 1 because the number is so big. Why? Well it stumped me, as did trying to explain multiplication to her because it involved something more than addition; but what that more was was hard to show. Multiplication used addition but somehow also went beyond it. My daughter needed to use addition as an element of multiplication, not focus on addition whilst trying to do multiplication.

What Piaget became increasingly fascinated with was how we shift from absorption in the process of doing something (like addition) to being able to use the process as a stepping-stone to do something new (like multiplication). What initially immerses us, challenges us, takes up all our concentration slowly becomes obvious and easy. We are able to use it as a tool to do something new.

With multiplication, for example, we don't focus on the mechanics of doing the addition, but how many addition operations have been done. The individual action of counting suddenly becomes the co-ordinated action of using addition for something fresh. Suddenly we are able to work in chunks of three rather than having to count to three each time. Addition becomes a stepping-stone to multiplication.

This process gripped Piaget because it revealed the inner activity of cognitive development. The child does not just go from concrete world to abstract concept (as real doggie in the world is classified by the word concept dog), but then goes on to use the abstract concept as the base for new moves (for example, how dogs and cats are both animals). You can actually watch this happen.

Ask a child if there are more animals or dogs in figure 4.1. Chances are, if the child is under six years old, she will say there are more dogs than animals. She has got to grips with counting, and with dogs and cats, but not the fact that both dogs and cats are included in a larger category of animals. To do this, she would have to stop focusing on the dogs and cats and shift to what makes both dogs and cats animals. She would also have to shift from what things look like on the page, where it is clear that there are more dogs than anything else, to a more conceptual space where she works with dogs and cats as categories, with both being types of animals. Piaget called this process reflective abstraction.

Figure 4.1 'Are there more animals than dogs?'

Reflective abstraction – driver of the educational imagination

The reason why reflective abstraction is so exciting is because it opens out endless new vistas of development beyond the concrete and everyday world. Rather than work with how things combine, you start to work with how the combinations combine, and then with how the combinations of combinations combine, and then with how the combinations of combinations of combinations combine. (This resonates with the previous chapter's discussion of chunking into ever larger and more sophisticated networks).

Reflective abstraction is not an empty recursion like the 'thank you for the thank you' note I once sent to one of my obsessive compulsive friends who then sent me back a 'thank you for the thank you for the thank you' note (and confessed that although she found it funny she also just had to do it for what passes as peace of mind in her world.)

With reflective abstraction each higher level works with a set of principles different from those below it, but includes within it the basic operations of the previous level. You don't just repeat the same step, but you include the step and move to something higher, like shifting from addition to multiplication; or from naming cats and dogs to a higher concept of 'animals' that includes cats and dogs. Often you have to alter how you think about the step because the higher level reveals how restricted your earlier understanding was. You have to accommodate your earlier understanding to the changes and bring it in line with the higher level.

This enables you to get closer to the fullness of reality as you move increasingly further away from it. You are able to perform increasingly complex transformations that get closer and closer to what is the most complex of all, the fullness of reality, but to get there you become more and more abstract. Piaget was not interested in leaving reality, but getting closer to it.[21] Reflective abstraction reduced the gap between the possible and the necessary, because it increased the reach and sophistication of the possible, enabling it to get closer and closer to the way the world actually works. As Piaget put it, 'Knowing reality means constructing systems of transformations that correspond, more or less adequately, to reality' (Piaget, 1970, p. 15). Reflective abstraction is the key generating mechanism of the educational imagination. There is no other mechanism that catches the heart of its basic functioning more than reflective abstraction. It continually expands outwards and upwards into ever-richer worlds of possibility, but in doing so comes nearer and nearer to the fullness of reality; or in Piagetian terms, 'knowledge is a system of transformations that become progressively adequate' (Piaget, 1970, lecture one). It is not enough to know that dogs and cats are animals – we need to get to the stage of understanding all the levels contained within 'animalia'.

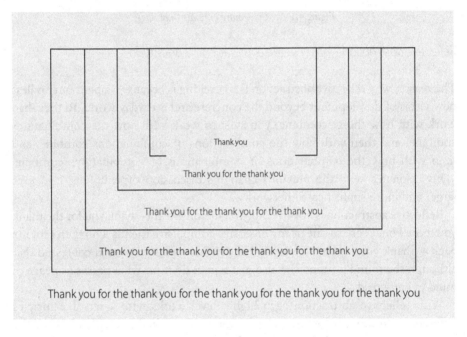

Figure 4.2 Recurring but empty recursion

From babe to sage

So just how many levels of cognitive development are there? If we continue to reflect and abstract upon a level, do we not land up in a world where there are infinite levels of development, each getting closer and closer to the fullness of reality but never quite reaching it? And what is the fullness of reality? Is it just physical reality, or do we have to include emotional and spiritual dimensions to the fullness? It is similar to Zeno's paradoxes (figure 4.3) that have delighted and frustrated philosophers for over two thousand years. We can start with the same problem Piaget delighted in giving to children, the space between point A and B, except what is at issue is not the number of possible paths, but the impossibility of ever reaching your end point. You start off by making it half way (to how the world works), but still have half the journey to go. However, the distance left can also be halved, and so on, with the result that you get closer and closer to your destination but never quite reach it because this ever-shrinking distance can always be halved.[22]

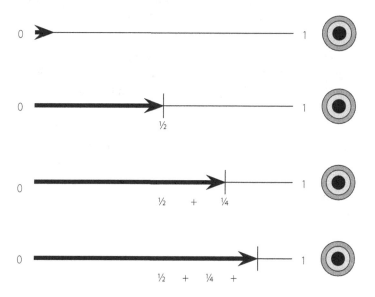

Figure 4.3 Zeno's paradox of arrow never hitting target, or of the possible never hitting the actual

Notice that this presents a very different model of the educational imagination from its stereotype, where, as we exercise our educational imaginations we are able to travel further and further to more and more exotic locations. On Zeno's model, the space we work in shrinks and shrinks as we get closer and closer to an end point, making the work of the imagination harder and harder within an increasingly confined space, with increasingly more intricate detail. At each level of cognitive development we get closer to the full complexity of the real, but there is always space for a new level of development in the infinite gap, no matter how small, between levels of development and the fullness of being. Do we eventually stop this ever intensifying process of reflective abstraction and just rest in the fullness of being, whatever that is supposed to be? Do we reach a point where it is impossible to perform the act of reflective abstraction, or where the act does not produce any new level, only more of the same, where necessity and possibility meet, not just in experiments but in our fully lived reality? Is there an end to the educational imagination? Piaget worked with four basic cognitive levels, each of which had many sub-levels or stages, but are there not many more levels waiting to take us way beyond the formal operational? Just as with the materiality of schools where we took all the schools of the world as our focus, should we not open out to all the levels of development human experience has shown us?

Let's put it rhetorically. Do you think Jesus, Mohammed, da Vinci, Einstein, Gandhi, Steve Jobs and Mandela stopped at the formal operational level where the rules of logic are used on the world? Two immediate responses spring to mind. The first is that they might have been highly developed in other areas that have little to do with cognitive development. This opens up the issue of there being different domains (lines or streams) of development. The second is that they might have moved beyond formal operational thinking into new and higher levels of thinking. We have to keep these two responses clear. Just because you show high levels of development does not mean this is necessarily in cognition. To get really close to the fullness of being, maybe you need to work both at reaching the highest level of cognitive development but then also try to get to the highest level of all the other lines of development as well, whether they be moral, emotional, aesthetic, kinaesthetic, linguistic, or whatever. Only then can you claim to have got closest to the infinity of the real because only then do you gain a purchase on all the different facets of the real, not only its logical components. The interior world of an individual student, which opened out at the beginning of this chapter, suddenly deepens and widens.

Believe it or not: undergraduates also develop

What would happen, for example, if we took university students as our focus, not little children? Would they not show levels of development very different from those described by Piaget? Take a fresh-faced, first-year humanities undergraduate student and put her next to a more worldly-wise third-year student. What happened in three years? It turns out that students go through a recognisable intellectual and emotional journey (Perry, 1970). Normally students start out with a strong sense of right and wrong imbibed from family and community. His or her own point of view is right, everyone else is wrong. The complex world of university life quickly makes them aware that there are many things they actually don't know about. Their dualistic world breaks open to the recognition of multiplicity, that there are things in the world they have not dreamt about, shattering their sense of obvious rightness. Initially, when they enter this world they just want to know which theory is right. Students often stop me when I try to get a debate going with a demand that I just tell them which view is correct. They quickly shift into a world where diversity dominates and tumble enthusiastically into an anything goes attitude. Every perspective is valid as a personal opinion. Within this sea of choice students eventually have to take a stand based on what they think, feel and believe. But what a student now believes is not the same as when she arrived, having undergone a process of doubt and expansion, resulting in her being able to make an informed choice based on a variety of attractive alternatives. This is not just a cognitive move, it's an ethical one where the student commits to an informed way of being and acting in the world and continues to refine her identity and values based on these commitments.[23]

Notice in the move from Piaget to Perry we have done two things. First, we have started to explore if there are levels beyond Piaget's four. Second, we have shifted from a focus on how a child's cognitive schema get closer to the necessities of the real world to the way a student self-actualises. It's about becoming everything you are capable of becoming rather than getting cognition closer to reality. Curiously, at higher levels of development, self-actualisation and getting closer to reality come together. Perry focused on undergraduate students and they certainly do not have the last word on levels of human development, given their struggle to assert who they are in a complex world, and given the limited sample of students (Western, middle class, white). We need to work with studies that focus on the full range of possible development, not just children or students and not just cognitive development.

Self-actualisation and self-transcendence

We find such a focus in the work of Abraham Maslow. He saw his work as a complement to Freud: 'It is as if Freud supplied us the sick half of psychology and we must now fill it out with the healthy half' (Maslow, 1968, p. 5). Maslow was interested in the best we could become, famously developing a hierarchy of needs in which the final level was self-actualisation. Rather than a cognitive line, he explored the needs human beings have and express. Maslow used highly developed individuals like Einstein who clearly had fulfilled their potential across a number of lines as his data source. You can check your own levels of self-actualisation by asking yourself the following 10 questions:

1. Do you (a) work with reality the way it is, or (d) fight for your version of it?
2. Do you (a) do what feels good and natural for you, or (d) do what others expect of you and pretend it's actually your own initiative?
3. Are you (a) focused on problems of society and other people, or (d) focused on your own problems but tell yourself they are of great importance to the world?
4. Do you (a) enjoy solitude, privacy and self-reflection, or (d) keep the TV on for company and/or have lots of friends around most of the time? Put differently, do you think that all your 500 Facebook friends are really your friends?
5. Are you (a) comfortable in silence with friends, or (d) continually feel the need to fill space with your wit, wisdom and gossip?

6. Do you (a) enjoy playing the games you did as a child, or (d) are you happy to leave the children doing their own thing while you drink beer and watch sport, or resent the men drinking beer and watching sport?
7. Do you (a) celebrate deep and profound experiences when they come along, or (d) deny any knowledge of such experiences and laugh dismissively at such accounts?
8. Do you (a) feel in tune with reality, or (d) must reality tune into your wavelength?
9. Do you (a) believe that people are essentially good and can be trusted, or (d) are just waiting for the chance to take advantage?
10. Do you (a) have deep and meaningful relationships with a few people, or (d) are known to be a slag or bastard, or suspected at least of having the tendency?
11. Is your sense of humour (a) philosophical, unhostile and good natured, or (d) sarcastic and crude?
12. Did you (a) try to answer the quiz honestly, or (d) try to score all 'a's even though it's a meaningless quiz meant only to demonstrate self-actualisation?

Of course you both answered honestly and scored 12/12. You can see from the quiz that self-actualised people are realistic about the world and themselves; focus on helping others and finding solutions to real concerns; are spontaneous both in thought and action; enjoy autonomy and solitude; continue to have freshness of appreciation; and enjoy peak experiences when they come around.

The problem was that the more Maslow researched fully self-actualised human beings, the more he realised he was at the tip of a new phenomenon that had more to do with self-transcendence than self-actualisation. In 1969, the year before he died, he established the Association for Transpersonal Psychology. He was interested in climactic peak experiences and more serene forms of contemplative plateau living. What opened out in front of Maslow just before his heart gave in was the massive treasure trove of transpersonal experience to be found in the spiritual psychologies of Taoism, Buddhism, Judaism, Christianity and Sufism. His own articulation of transpersonal levels of development was an inevitable hodgepodge, put together in a rush of excitement and energy, called Theory Z. Here are 10 of the 24 characteristics (Maslow, 1971, pp. 283–294).

- They speak easily, normally, naturally and unconsciously the language of Being … the language of poets, of mystics, of seers, of profoundly religious men.
- They see sacredness in all things at the same time that they also see them at the practical, everyday … level.
- They seem somehow to recognise each other and to come to almost instant intimacy and mutual understanding even upon first meeting.

- They are more responsive to beauty.
- Not only are such people lovable as are all of the most self-actualizing people, but they are also more awe-inspiring, more 'unearthly', more godlike, more 'saintly' ... more easily revered.
- Transcenders, I think, should be less afraid of 'nuts' and 'kooks' than are other self-actualizers, and thus are more likely to be good selectors of creators (who sometimes look nutty or kooky) ... [T]o value a William Blake type takes, in principle, a greater experience with transcendence and therefore a greater valuation of it.
- They are more apt to regard themselves as carriers of talent, instruments of the transpersonal, temporary custodians so to speak of a greater intelligence ... This means a certain peculiar kind of objectivity or detachment toward themselves.
- Transcenders ... would have ... more of the fascinations that we see in children who get hypnotised by the colours in a puddle, by the raindrops dripping down a windowpane, by the smoothness of skin, or the movements of a caterpillar.
- Transcenders have throughout history seemed spontaneously to prefer simplicity and to avoid luxury, privilege, honours, and possessions.
- I cannot resist expressing what is only a vague hunch; namely, the possibility that my transcenders seem to me somewhat more apt to be Sheldonian ectomorphs [lean, nerve-tissue dominated body-types] while my less-often-transcending self-actualizers seem more often to be mesomorphic [muscular body-types].

As I read this I was struck by just how tentative Maslow was about his theory. He candidly admits that he has only carefully talked to and observed three or four dozen subjects, and that he has not been able to verify the reliability of his information or ensure the representativeness of his sample. All the references, bar two, are from his own work. Before he could take this new area of transpersonal psychology into formally verified science, he died. But what we see opening before us with him is a vast territory far beyond the developmental levels with which Piaget worked. So whenever you use Maslow's hierarchy of needs, please use the one that includes transcendence (figure 4.4).

Maslow did not provide a fully worked-out exposition of transcendence. The person who has become famous for synthesising this vast space is the American, Ken Wilber. He is in no way at the same level as Piaget and Freud, or Jung for that matter. Much of his work comes from synthesising the cosmic traditions of spiritual mysticism and his own personal experiences, not from a lifetime of engagement in research. But that said, he does provide a simple overview of the field that both uses Piaget and places Piaget within the broader field of human developmental studies.

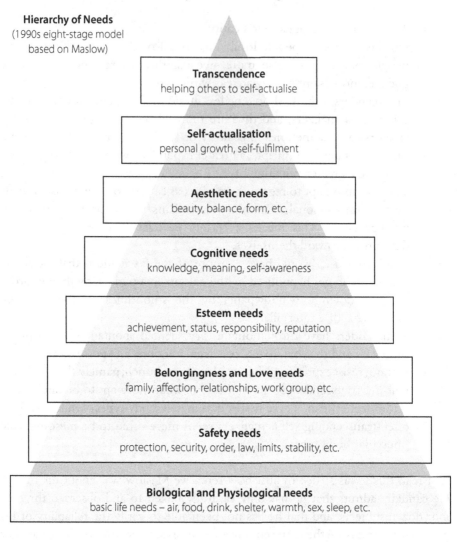

Hierarchy of Needs
(1990s eight-stage model
based on Maslow)

Transcendence
helping others to self-actualise

Self-actualisation
personal growth, self-fulfilment

Aesthetic needs
beauty, balance, form, etc.

Cognitive needs
knowledge, meaning, self-awareness

Esteem needs
achievement, status, responsibility, reputation

Belongingness and Love needs
family, affection, relationships, work group, etc.

Safety needs
protection, security, order, law, limits, stability, etc.

Biological and Physiological needs
basic life needs – air, food, drink, shelter, warmth, sex, sleep, etc.

Figure 4.4 Model of Maslow's eight-stage hierarchy of needs

Wilber was able to do what Maslow only glimpsed at: engage the world's spiritual traditions with a sympathetic integrating eye for what they tell us about advanced levels of human development; not how they have resulted in pillage, looting, burning at the stake, and condemnation of most of humanity to eternal damnation. What would you find if you took the whole world's experiences of human development as your brief: East and West, North and South, ancient and modern, sacred and secular? What would you find if you tried to explore the heights of development we can reach inside ourselves?

You can find an early account of his synthesis in the humbly titled *A Brief History of Everything* (2007) or the more detailed and impressive *Sex, Ecology and Spirit* (2000), in which he outlines four levels of human development beyond the formal operational: vision-logic, psychic, subtle, and causal. What for Piaget was mystical gibberish and for Maslow a chaotic list of 24 characteristics is for Wilber a clearly demarcated set of levels to climb, each with a number of different lines articulated by different researchers (cognitive – Piaget; needs – Maslow; moral – Kohlberg), its own pedagogic strategies and sets of educational practices. Like Piaget and the process of reflective abstraction, each level is approached by taking the previous level as its working base and producing something new above that both including and transcending its earlier version in a three-step process. First, you enter the new level of development and identify or fuse with that level. Second, on reflection, you start to recognise that there are problems and begin to disassociate and differentiate from the level. Third, you begin to see how to use the problems and practices of the level as an abstracted base to move to a new level. And this happens not just in one dimension like cognition, but in many dimensions, all at different rates and intensities, depending on the individual. The world inside a student is slightly more complex than all the desks of the world.

The problem is that it's not so easy to demonstrate what these higher levels actually are because they are hard to recognise if you have not been there yourself, and not many of us have hit these higher stages across different lines in any sustained way. When we examined some examples of children answering questions about moving from point A to B, or about dogs and cats and animals, you did not struggle because you have already gone through these levels and intuitively knew the answers. But once we get into these transpersonal levels much of it sounds paradoxical or kooky, not helped at all by the large number of real crazies out there. You only really get it once you have transformed your consciousness, but then it's an open question as to whether you have gone crazy yourself.

What has helped to chart these wild waters is a combination of increased scientific and scholarly scrutiny on the one hand and the opening out of local and historical practices to international awareness, allowing a more critical and cosmopolitan awareness. This has enabled a synthetic account of levels and lines of development that ranges across the full spectrum rather than stopping in middle adolescence (Piaget), undergraduate student (Perry), or early transcendence (Maslow). Using Wilber as our close guide, what would you experience as a self-mover through these different levels and lines (figure 4.5)?

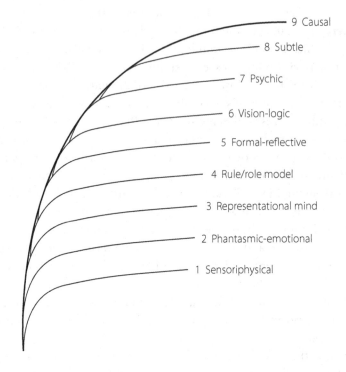

Figure 4.5 Basic structures of consciousness

I follow chapters 10–13 of a *Brief History of Everything* closely in the following account.

1. *Sensori-physical*: As an infant you don't yet know the difference between inside and outside: your thumb and blanket are part of the same experiential matrix. Your physical self and the physical world are fused, or in Piaget's phrasing 'The self is here material' (Wilber, 2007, p. 158). It's true that self and world are one, but not in a transcendent way, more in a primary narcissistic way that is very shallow. You cannot take on the role of the other and see the world through your mother's eye: how can you when the world is you and you are the world? Immediate impressions dominate in a unitary flow. Around four months you start to differentiate yourself from the world. Sucking your thumb somehow feels different from sucking a blanket and there is a strange difference between the two. Mahler calls this the hatching phase (Wilber, 2007, p. 162) where the physical self emerges from primal existence. With this emergence of a physical self a new level opens out that builds on the base of a physical self, but is different from it.

2. *Phantasmic-emotional*: You have a realistic boundary to your physical being, but have not yet established boundaries to your emotional self. Your

emotions are fused or identified with those around you, especially your mother. Again this is not deep love. It's still narcissistic and you treat the world as an emotional extension of yourself. What you feel, the whole world feels. You are not being selfish here, you are not thinking just about yourself; it's more that your own perspective is the only perspective around, your own emotions and vital life feelings flood the world. Between 15 and 24 months the emotional self begins to differentiate from the emotional environment and you experience the birth or emergence of your psychological self (Wilber, 2007, p. 165). You wake up as a separate self in a separate world. With the emergence of an emotional and physical self a new level opens up that builds on this base, but is different from it.

3. *Representational mind*: You have a realistic boundary to your physical and emotional self, but have not yet established what your mental or conceptual self is. As you enter a linguistic world, symbols and concepts take on increasing importance. You use symbols to name what is most important to you (Ma, Da, Hadeeda in Lexi's case). Around four years of age you begin to grasp how concepts work. The word cat is different from 'meouw mouw' and Ticky. You are not just a bundle of sensations, impulses and emotions but also a set of symbols and concepts (Wilber, 2007, p. 169). It's a new world where you can think about the past and anticipate the future, where it occurs to you with a jolt that your parents will die and that you will die, where you remember what it was like to be a baby and long for its peaceful cocoon. Around six or seven you begin to realise that symbols and concepts give you purchase on a whole world of mental rules and social roles you did not suspect existed. A new level opens up that builds on the emergence of a physical, emotional and mental self, but is different from it.

4. *Rule-role mind*: You have a realistic boundary to your physical, emotional and mental self but have not yet established your social self or the rules by which you operate with mental concepts and emotional states. Slowly you begin to be able to put yourself in other people's shoes and imagine what it is like to view things from their perspective. Your view is not the only view of the world and you shift quickly from a pre-conventional stance where you did not really understand the order of the world to a conventional world where you uncritically take on, in the most conformist of ways, what your mother, father and teachers say is right and wrong. Your moral line of reasoning shifts dramatically into a law and order phase. Now that you can see what their perspective is, you take it right into yourself. Your cognitive development shifts from pre-operational to concrete operational where you are able to work logically with the world so long as it is concretised for you. You know that when you pour water from a wide, short glass into a tall, thin glass the volume of water remains

the same even though the level is higher in the thin glass. When you are shown a video of your younger self saying that the tall, thin glass has more water than the wide, short glass, you will laugh and deny that it was you or insist that some kind of trick is being played because it is obvious that the amount has not changed. You are not caught out by how things appear, can hold more than one variable in your mind at the same time, and show a continued decrease in narcissistic and egoistic behaviour as you shift to more socio-centric ways of being. You fuse yourself with the roles and rules into which you are inserted. You are a pleasure to teach at primary school because you want to know what the rule is so you can follow it. You wait for your teacher so you can carry her bag. Around the end of primary school and the beginning of high school something starts to happen to you. It's as if you don't want to listen to us any more, you start to have your own thoughts based on possible worlds. The given rules and roles are not enough; you want to experiment with new possibilities, not old givens. A new level opens up that builds on the emergence of a physical, emotional, mental and rule/role driven self, but is different from it.

5. *Formal-reflexive*: You have a realistic boundary to your physical, emotional, mental and rule/role self, but have not yet established what this new world of abstract possibility and potentiality offers. You begin to think about thinking. You can do more than try out various concrete combinations on a table, you can hold all the possible combinations of something in your head and work from the possible to the actual. Possible worlds open out to your imagination. You start to judge the rules and roles you followed so enthusiastically just a few years before. You start to criticise your parents, teachers and culture and embrace counter stances, completely transforming your identity and look. What is most important is that you look different, listen to different music and hang out with different looking friends who must look the same as you. Hopefully, if you have done a good job of integrating the previous levels, these new roles and ideas take you away from an exclusive identity with conventionality into a more world-centric position where you ask not only what is right and fair for you and your group, but for all people. From being completely unaware of the world as a separate entity, you now have the whole world as your focus and a post-conventional attitude begins to emerge about how to live within it. But with the questioning of conventional roles and rules comes the strong likelihood of an identity crisis where you start to search for who you are beyond all the roles and rules you absorbed in the past. What also emerges is a deep relativism of the 'anything goes' variety, where everyone is entitled to their point of view, especially you. But you begin to sense that this is too easy a position, that there are better and worse ways of living and thinking; and that you have to start synthesising and integrating as well as

just allowing everyone their own freedom. A new set of possibilities opens out that looks for holistic patterns and tries to live by them.

6. *Vision-logic*: You have a realistic grasp of your physical, emotional, mental, rule/role and abstract/alternative self, but have not yet established how all these differences and possibilities hold together in an integrated and holistic manner. You are not only thinking about thinking, but about all the patterns and networks thrown up by thinking about thinking. The embrace of alternative possibilities has left you with a massive set of openings that is dizzying: there is no pillow to rest your head and say 'I got it'. And if it's an 'emo' alternative existence you have embraced, then your pillow will be too wet anyway. You can experience it as a wonderful embrace of different perspectives or as a dangerous paralysis where all is possible, but nothing is better than anything else. At the heart of it you have the task of becoming authentic rather than merely alternative, of finding your own authentic being in the world (as Heidegger describes it) or of self-actualising (as Maslow puts it). The full weight of existing in the world without comforting illusions comes to bear. You have reached your three As – autonomous, authentic and actualised – but somehow it all feels a little meaningless, given that you are not going to be around for very long and all you do is going to fade and crumble anyway, just like that face of yours staring at you in the mirror. But occasionally you have a different experience that takes you out of your triple-A rating into a broader and deeper awareness. Like Maslow, you are not really sure what that is, but it involves some kind of intensification of awareness of Being, not your being, but of all Being.

7. *Psychic*: You have a realistic grasp of your triple-A self, but beyond this lies a new world hinted at by occasional peak experiences. The most common is a form of nature mysticism when a pleasant walk through the mountains or forests suddenly turns immersive. Natural beauty intensifies from being enjoyable to astonishing. Your perspective deepens, colours intensify, sounds and silence magnify and you forget all your own existential crap as the exquisiteness of existence overtakes you. This happens a lot in Cape Town, by the way, where Table Mountain has a lot to answer for, although recorded cases of nature mysticism by taking the cable car are hard to find, so most tourists do not quite get it. As you fuse more and more with these kinds of experiences you de-centre from your own existence and become intensely aware of the world and all its being, whether this be stone, plant, animal or human. This also accounts, by the way, for the large number of vegans in Cape Town and the refusal to participate in the mass suffering of animals across our world. What happens on the Cape Flats is a different matter, of course. A powerful sensitivity to the environment takes on a lived and ethical dimension. You start to see the world differently. Animals and plants take on

individual identities that are precious and obvious to you. You become more aware of and sensitive to who people are, what they are doing and what they are going through, often just in a revealing touch or glance. People's individual natures shine out of them, while perception of physical ugliness disappears and is replaced by an intense seeing of character. But as these sensitivities increase you begin to develop a more subtle sensitivity to energies beyond nature. These energies sometimes take on a life of their own.

8. *Subtle*: As you stabilise in a new world of Being as well as the old world of existence, you begin to work with subtle energies in their own right, not as they express themselves through a plant, animal or human. You start to become adept at seeing, feeling and participating in the energies on their own terms. You begin to experience internal luminosities, sounds and thoughts and emotions that are of the state itself rather than attached to an object. Feelings of love and compassion flood through you without thoughts of someone you love. You experience forces in their own terms. If you are a Christian, for example, you don't experience Christ as a man with a beard and white tunic coming towards you with a soulful but still sexy smile; you experience a flooding of pure love or grace that has a subtle rather than physical structure. As you become able to hold yourself in these states something beckons behind these subtle energies, something more silent, emptier, but somehow also more full.

9. *Causal*: To reach and hold onto states of psychic and subtle awareness you have to become more and more adept at silencing yourself and opening out to the energies both inside and outside you. You begin to be attracted to actual silence rather than what silence enables you to experience, no matter how subtle, beautiful and profound the energies. Rather than being an empty opening or clearing that allows existence to dance, you start to stay in the clearing in its own terms and when this happens the fullness of being hits you without any attachment, image, energy or name. The Isness of Being hums as a vast freedom. You experience it as a timeless, spaceless, objectless creative ground from which everything springs, so it is sometimes called the causal level. It's the state that allows other states to arise from it. Reflective abstraction finally meets its match. The problem is that it is a really hard state to reach, never mind sustain, but it is also a state that's pretty empty in its own terms. You have experienced the watcher rather than used it to watch, so what? The challenge that arises is to hold the state while going about your everyday life and so a new challenge opens out to you even though you have travelled into the depths of your being to the point where you have experienced pure Being. It gets you up off your backside and into the world.

Even though you have stabilised in a transpersonal world at psychic, subtle and causal levels, what most attracts you are not these states, but living life, of getting back into the world at all its levels, physical, emotional, mental, social, abstract, existential, psychic, subtle and causal, and giving it your best shot (not that you would now use a language that involves shooting.) It's not that you don't experience desire, love, anger, hope or sadness. A journey through these levels does not leach you of all that is human, but it makes you experience them with a new intensity and clarity. Spend some time with Bishop Desmond Tutu, Nelson Mandela (RIP) or the Dalai Lama and you will quickly find they are the most intense and character filled human beings around. Jonathan Jansen has a similar way about him. They would all resonate with most of the account above, but of far more importance to them is what they have done in the world and how they have answered the call to work lovingly, intelligently and critically on a difficult but beautiful planet called Earth. And Tau, circling above us, would hopefully nod hir head, if sie has one.

Obviously I have given a highly simplified tour of what is an astonishingly complex process and normally the above account comes with all sorts of hedges, qualifications, intricacies and alternatives. But what I want you to experience is the stretching of your educational imagination. First, I want your mind to stretch from a school outwards to all the schools of the world. Second, to shift focus inside the school to all the elements that make it up. Third, to shift from the smallest material elements of schooling to the smallest functional process of learning at a neuronal level and its behavioural correlate found in working and long-term memory. Fourth, to shift from this micro-focus on the intersection between brain/mind to the incredible developmental range human beings have that takes us on a journey from the basic act of working out that our bodies exist; to entry into a logical and social world; and then into the most transcendent of human experiences, all potentially contained in the form of an individual student sitting at a defaced desk with a grin on her face.

What this fourth expansion should do is open you up to the realisation that pedagogic techniques extend far beyond getting us to read, write and think in logical and critical ways. Yoga is a pedagogy, as is meditation and prayer. Sri Aurobindo and Patanjali's texts on Yoga are pedagogic texts as are Plotinus' *Enneads*, Augustine's *On the Trinity* and St John of the Cross' *Dark Night of the Soul*. I have tracked the Western types of these pedagogies in *Ladders of Beauty* (2007), but here want to emphasise that the educational imagination reaches upwards into the heights of human spiritual practice. For at the highest of the high there are pedagogic practices that enable our reaching and at the heart of this reaching lies the process of reflective abstraction, the queen activity of the educational imagination.

Figure 4.6 Higher levels provide expanding insight

The interior world of an individual student might be a wonder to behold, but it only exists as a part of a human world that gives her the language, tools and experiences to explore an internal world. It is to this human world that we now turn, not to understand how humanity works, but to understand how education intersects with humanity at its broadest and most particular levels. We might have, in this chapter, reached the heights within our interior, but what of the heights we have reached as a human species; and how has education helped us arrive there?

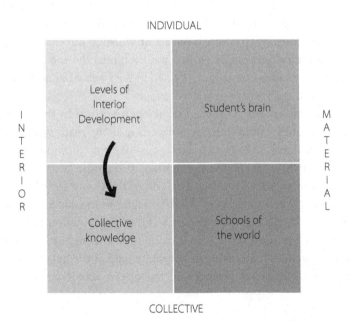

Figure 4.7 Shift from interior levels of development to the collective knowledge of the world

Chapter 5

History of the world in a child

The strange thing about a child is that she is able to learn, in the space of twelve to fifteen years, what has taken collective humanity twenty thousand years and more to work out. We were struggling with how zero and the decimal system worked two thousand years ago, and now we get it in grade 1. Maybe the interior development of an individual learner shows up, in miniature and speeded-up form, the whole history of human development? Now that is an exciting thought. In working with one student you have the chance to recapitulate and then take further the development of our species. We don't really know what Neanderthal men were thinking, but maybe we can find it in the earlier levels of childhood development. A child, sitting on that plastic chair at a trapezoid table, is actually the missing link between prehistoric humankind and us. It's not only a beautiful world of interior depth that we find inside a child; it's the whole history of us as a species.

Ontogeny recapitulates phylogeny

This was the real reason Piaget studied children. Through them he felt he had access to the genesis and sequence of knowledge development in our species. Piaget studied the concepts of space, time, causality, number and logical classes as they develop in the minds of children because they revealed in individual knowledge code the history of knowledge development. Unlike Tau, who would have to float above us for a hundred thousand years, watching us slowly and painfully mastering the massive gap between the necessities of existence and the possible ways of dealing with it, Piaget could get the same view in miniature and individual form by working with children. The idea is enormously seductive and has been around in different forms since the ancient Greeks. Here is Herbert Spencer, writer of one of the most popular and long-lasting educational textbooks in nineteenth-century England:

> If there be an order in which the human race has mastered its various kinds of knowledge, there will arise in every child an aptitude to acquire these kinds of knowledge in the same order (Spencer, 1861, p. 5).

This idea is caught in the dismaying phrase 'ontogeny recapitulates phylogeny'; the development of the individual shows in miniature the development of the species. The reason we go through stages of biological development as individuals (ontogeny) has to do with repeating the way our species evolved over time (phylogeny). If our species added a key new feature as it evolved, you will be able to find it in the development of an individual, especially in the earlier phases. If we assume that humans are the most developed of species (a very dangerous assumption), then it stands to reason that in our individual development from embryo to adult we shall find in compressed form evidence of all the earlier life forms in our past. Allow me to state that this is a crude and hyperbolic form: study the developmental processes of one human being and within it you will find a compressed record of the history of all life since its origin. Look at the early stages of a human embryo and you will find indicators of gills and tails from our evolutionary past as fish and monkeys.

Stephen Jay Gould provides a fascinating account of this idea in *Ontogeny and Phylogeny* and I don't want to go into the details; first because he has already done it better than I ever could, but second because it gets us away from our focus on education. There are, however, two principles of the recapitulation thesis that are vital for us in understanding how it speaks to education: terminal addition and condensation.

Terminal addition simply states that a new stage of development is added onto the end of previous existing levels, much as a new floor is added to an existing building. What makes us as human beings, supposedly higher in the evolutionary sequence than other life forms, is that we have added extra stages on top. In terms of figure 5.1, we have increasingly added more stages onto 'a', eventually getting to 'a', 'b', 'c' and 'd'. But, we have not increased our life span to make room for the extra stages, so we have to pack them in by running through the stages more quickly (or by jumping them.) We can see this in figure 5.1: stage 'a' becomes increasingly shorter as the number of stages increases (Gould, 1977, pp. 74–75).

This idea has been disproven biologically in this form, but it's not so clear that it does not work in terms of knowledge evolution: is it not possible that the way we learn a subject is in much the same form as it developed over time, only we have had to condense the process? Initially all we learnt was 'a', but once we mastered 'a' we found out about 'b'. This resulted in having to learn 'b' as well as 'a', and then we found out about 'c' and 'd', and so on. The only problem is that we still need time to learn 'a' as well as 'b', 'c' and 'd', and we only have a limited life to do it in. At some stage we have to stop learning and get working.[24] Spencer thought the way a subject (like mathematics) historically worked with its difficulties, overcame them and then moved on to higher, more difficult areas, which again presented complications that were overcome, is similar to the way we individually learn the subject.

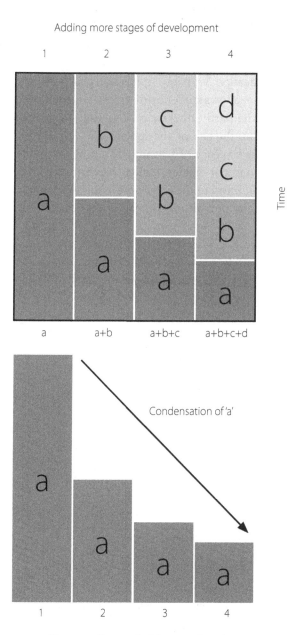

Figure 5.1 Terminal addition and condensation

It is a very dangerous assumption, but one that has had a massive impact on the way we teach and learn. Strangely, the impact has partly been about lifting our foot off the accelerator in terms of learning and allowing students time to explore problem areas themselves in a creative way.

If we individually learn a subject in the same way our species worked through the process historically, then we must allow our students the same space to explore and trust that they will also find their way through to the answer, just as our species did. We might nudge them on the way by constructing the learning environment carefully, but if we are treading a well-worn path our species has already taken, we can trust the process of exploration to take the student all the way.

Much progressive education, with its emphasis on problem solving in a learner-centred environment that allows students to explore creatively an open issue with minimal guidance, can be partly tracked back to this assumption. But as more and more was added onto the end of the subject – 'e', 'f', 'g', 'h', 'i' and 'j' – the pressure built to increase the pace of learning, resulting in a modern curriculum where so much is packed into it that it is almost impossible to imagine a problem-solving student tinkering about in the classroom, experimenting with alternatives and dead ends in the slow pursuit of an answer the teacher (and the Internet) already knows.

Take a look at figure 5.2, which shows the development of mathematical concepts over the last ten thousand years (horizontal axis) and the age at which the concept is learnt in the United Kingdom (vertical axis) (Mesoudi, 2011). Notice any correlation?

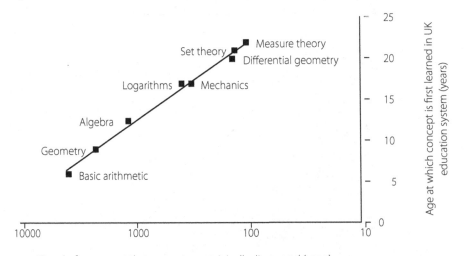

Figure 5.2 Subject ontogeny recapitulating subject phylogeny?

Is it possible that the way we learn mathematics over twenty years (subject ontogeny) recapitulates the way mathematics has developed over ten thousand years (subject phylogeny)? Notice how more and more concepts get added on later and later, resulting in the student having to learn more and more in the twenty years allocated. But the same massive addition of concepts is happening in science, biology, history and geography. It's a seductive idea, but as with any seduction, it is often built on untruths. This can be seen in figure 5.2 with set theory, which is a very late development in mathematics, but has been used in many programmes as one of the founding conceptual bases of mathematics learnt in primary school. So it cannot be time of discovery that gives the secret to the order in which concepts are learnt at a subject level. But that does not mean that the sequence of discovery over time does not, in obscured form, reveal the principle. Spencer did not claim that we have to follow the order of discovery of concepts in our school curriculum. For him it was subtler than that. It's a principle that he articulated in three currently under-rated classics: *First Principles* (1862), *Principles of Sociology* (1882–1898) and *On Education* (1861). The person he got it from was Von Baer. And the principle is individuation.

Hierarchies and individuation

Recapitulation stated that an individual organism repeats the adult stages of previous developmental forms and then adds new developments on at the end (terminal addition) and makes time and space for these additions by compressing previous levels (condensation). Von Baer offered a different organising principle through his study of embryonic development. We start with a general and undifferentiated state that is common to all and, through a process of differentiation, become more individual and unique. Rather than go through specific early stages that replicate earlier adult levels where each state adds to the next on a hierarchical ladder, we go from a simple and homogenous state to a complex and individuated state. This means in principle that general features appear earlier than specialised features with the implication that specialised features develop out of more all-purpose features. What this means is that the only time there is a similarity between different animals is in their embryonic stage, because it is here that functions are still to be differentiated. Human beings, for example, do not go through the full history of all previous adult life forms from which the species has evolved. Rather they go through stages of individuation, starting in an undifferentiated 'soup' and increasingly emerge with more and more distinctiveness and particularity. We look similar to other species at early levels because we are all undifferentiated, not because we are going through a 'fish' stage. But as we differentiate, we take different paths. We are not different from fish because we added extra levels of development onto fish; we are different because we took a different path. Both we and fish developed, but in different ways.

The reason why I am briefly going through Von Baer's critique of recapitulation is that it breaks a certain tendency of thought that works in a linear and hierarchical way. The recapitulation principles of terminal addition and condensation keep the same sequence of development with the only possibility of change coming from adding something to the end point. It's the difference between the two following images in figure 5.3.

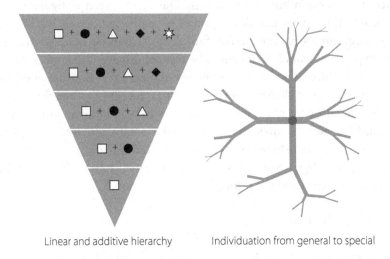

Linear and additive hierarchy   Individuation from general to special

Figure 5.3 Hierarchy and individuation

Note that with individuation the shift is from a more general undifferentiated state (starting with the circle and thick lines) to increasingly differentiated states (thin lines). The second key move Von Baer makes is to argue that there is more than one type of organisation and that each type is distinctive to the others. These types cannot be put into some kind of hierarchy as each is fundamentally different. Each type, in its own terms, shifts from undifferentiated to specialised by following its own logic, not by recapitulating the logic of previous forms. Each goes from simple to complex, but in its own distinct way. This results in a branching out logic rather than a single ladder.

It's a key insight for an educational imagination learning how to work with different types of levels. Human beings are not the highest species because we added extra levels on top of other species. We took our own path of differentiation and individuation that has led us to where we are now. Other species are on their own paths of individuation. They have not somehow become stuck because they have not added the same level we have on top of the other levels. That is simple human arrogance. They are chasing their own lines of individuation with their own higher levels that are not ours.

It's a view that breaks us out of assuming that maths or science should be organised in the same the way as history or geography. Each subject goes its own way, with its own set of differentiations that make it unique. That is why each subject produces experts who are different and who act, think and feel differently about the world because each subject goes off on its own individuating path. To expect every subject to reach a higher level that looks exactly how the higher levels of mathematics and science looks is dangerous. Von Baer's concept of individuation through differentiation has a lot to offer us in education and one of the people who saw this most clearly was Spencer.

Spencer: from simple to complex

Spencer was as famous in the late nineteenth century as Michel Foucault was in the late twentieth. Foucault gave us 'power' as a general organising principle through which to see the world. Derrida gave us 'deconstruction', Sartre 'existentialism' and John Dewey 'pragmatism'. Sadly, we have mostly forgotten Spencer, who gave us evolution and progress as the guiding principle of all reality, whether it was physics, biology, psychology or education. As with Foucault's power, if you understood the first principles of Spencer's system then the whole world unlocked for you. The principle was that all reality, not just life forms, moved from the simple and undifferentiated to the distinct and complex, but with different subjects taking different paths.

> Now, we propose in the first place to show that this law of organic progress is the law of all progress. Whether it be in the development of the Earth, in the development of Life upon its surface, the development of Society, of Government, of Manufactures, of Commerce, of Language, Literature, Science, Art, this same evolution of the simple into the complex, through a process of continuous differentiation, holds throughout. From the earliest traceable cosmical changes down to the latest results of civilization, we shall find that the transformation of the homogeneous into the heterogeneous is that in which Progress essentially consists (Spencer, 1857, pp. 446–447).

Simple homogenous things come together as an aggregate and this meeting causes differentiation of the various elements into components that are integrated into a more complex and coherent heterogeneous whole. These complex wholes can also compound, causing higher levels of differentiation and integration, resulting in continuing levels of development and progress that show increased adaptive functional capacity. A single simple element can perform only a highly limited range of actions, while a complex differentiated whole can respond in different but co-ordinated ways to the complexity of the environment by developing internal complexity. Differences are connected in highly organised ways, resulting in specialisation of functions. This in turn produces interdependence as each specialised function has to rely on others to do their bit. If the integration is not held in the face of environmental and internal pressures, then the complex whole can disintegrate. There is no inevitability to integration: times will arise when disintegrating pressures overwhelm the attempt to integrate and collapse becomes possible. These principles are applicable to all aspects of reality.

Spencer argued that the education of the child should go 'through a process like that which the mind of humanity at large has gone through. The truths of number, of form, of relationship in position, were all originally drawn from objects; and to present these truths to the child in the concrete is to let him learn them as the race learned them' (Spencer, 1861).

It seems, at a superficial level, Spencer is saying that if the 'race' learnt maths from basic arithmetic, through algebra and geometry to measure theory, then so should the child. But he is not saying that. He is pointing to a progression that works, not in terms of the sequence of historical concepts but of the shift from the simple to the complex, from the concrete to the abstract, and from the empirical to the rational (Spencer, 1861, p. 153). These all work with climbing levels, which is the major focus of this book, and, like Piaget, Spencer is a master of the climbing device in ways that speak directly to education.

It's at this deeper level that the way our species engaged with knowledge plays out in the individual child, not only or mainly in the sequence of topics. For Spencer the question of what should be in a school curriculum does not only revolve around mimicking the social and cultural history of humanity. He puts this into six education principles and I follow him closely in the list that follows:

1. Education should proceed from the simple to the complex, or from the homogenous to the heterogeneous, from the single to the combined and this should happen inside subjects and also in the ensemble of subjects, starting with a few simple and general subjects at the beginning and moving on to more subjects of increasing complexity later.

2. Lessons should go from the concrete to the abstract. It is important to distinguish the difference between simple/complex on the one hand, and concrete/abstract on the other. When a generalisation is made from many concrete particulars, it simplifies the many elements into one whole. Does this mean that because a generalisation is a simplification it should come first? Spencer pointed out that only 'after many single truths have been acquired does the generalization ease the memory and help the reason' (Spencer, 1861, p. 121). There are two processes at play here. First, a move from simple particulars to a more complex whole; and second, the complex whole finding an ordering relation between the various particulars. It is this abstract ordering that creates a simplification effect, not for each simple particular but for the complex whole.

3. With these two principles in place, he puts forward the recapitulation thesis for education: 'As the mind of humanity placed in the midst of phenomena

and striving to comprehend them, has, after endless comparisons, speculations, experiments, and theories, reached its present knowledge of each subject by a specific route; it may rationally be inferred that the relationship between mind and phenomena is such as to prevent this knowledge from being reached by any other route; and that as each child's mind stands in this same relationship to phenomena, they can be accessible to it only through the same route. Hence in deciding upon the right method of education, an enquiry into the method of civilization will help' (Spencer, 1861, pp. 123–124). Notice Spencer says method of civilisation, not order of topics in some sort of magical series. So what is the method of civilisation for Spencer? He gives an indication in the fourth principle.

4. A leading fact in human progress is that every science evolved out of its corresponding art. It results from the necessity we are under, both individually and as a race, of reaching the abstract by way of the concrete, that there must be practice and an accruing experience with its empirical generalisations before there can be science. Science is organised knowledge and before knowledge can be organised some of it must first be possessed (Spencer, 1861, p. 124). Every study should have a purely experimental introduction and only after an ample fund of observations has been accumulated should reasoning begin. Hence, the fourth principle: every branch of instruction should proceed from the empirical to the rational. If a curriculum is set up according to these first four principles, then a child should trace the way humankind reached knowledge by repeating the process of discovery, not by being told the content.

5. In doing this, pleasurable excitement will be encouraged in students, rather than the boredom forced by rote learning.

From theory to practice: examples of how not to do it

It is sadly the case, however, that educators under the influence of evolution at the end of the nineteenth century tended to go for a more literal version of recapitulation in which the school curriculum was ordered in the same sequence as the history of Western humanity. Gould gives a particularly humorous account of the results in Germany and the USA. Ziller and Rein, the only two professors of pedagogy in Germany in the 1880s, developed a primary school curriculum based on cultural epochs. Ziller provided the principles and inspiration, Rein the hard graft of converting the dream into eight volumes of actual curriculum. The principle was that

> [t]he mental development of the child corresponds in general to the chief phases in the development of his people or of mankind. The mind development of the child, therefore, cannot be better furthered than when he receives his

mental nourishment from the general development of culture as it is laid down in literature and history. Every pupil should, accordingly, pass successively through each of the chief epochs of the general mental development of mankind suitable to his stage of development (Gould, 1977, p. 150).

Gould notes that this worked fairly well for history, literature and moral education, but not so effectively for science, biology and mathematics. Were you supposed to teach the four humours and alchemy before modern biology and chemistry, that the Earth was flat before teaching it is round, that the sun moved round the Earth before reversing it, or that the number system should work with a base of 60 (the Babylonian numeral system) before moving on to a base 10 system? Ziller did recognise the difficulty and recommended that modern science and mathematics be taught logically, but that its examples should be drawn from the cultural epoch the child is currently studying. As Gould sardonically noted, this meant the teaching of geology and meteorology while hearing tales of Noah and the flood (Gould, 1977, p. 151) and considering mammals while the animals walked in two by two (could not help my own absurd addition). American applications of recapitulation used similar solutions and taught maths and science using examples from the historical and literary epoch organising the year. For example, McMurray from the University of Illinois designed the following curriculum in the late nineteenth century. First graders had, as a literary and cultural focus point, Anderson's *The Fir Tree*. Science looked at white pine trees, numeracy involved counting the number of pine needles and music used 'High in the Top of the Old Pine Tree'. Gould's delight in recounting this absurdity mounts as he goes on to describe how third graders, absorbed in *Robinson Crusoe*, would be drawing a stalk of wheat, counting the number of grains in a head of wheat and cheerfully singing 'When the Corn Begins to Sprout' (Gould, 1977, p. 152). Why *Robinson Crusoe*? Because the text catches our initial existence as savages, and what could be better for little savages than to imagine what it's like to be a savage. Johnny, sitting at his increasingly defaced table, could do with some savagery education.

This failure of the educational imagination is funny, but no funnier I suspect than what we are currently doing with multiple intelligence theory or neuro-linguistic programming. But what recapitulation did do, even though it died an explicit death as a biological theory, was provide strong support for the progressivist ideal of child-centred education in two related ways. First, it encouraged an integrated curriculum based on themes or issues; and second, it encouraged a learner-centred approach where the teacher did not have to do anything more than facilitate the process of discovery. Why? Because the child was in any case going to go automatically through the stages of development, best do it in a natural way just as nature and culture intended. Start off with exploration and open questions and allow the child to make the same moves that we did as a human species. Through mistakes the child will learn as we all did. Best of all, because as a species we have done it countless times before, it will somehow be easier. And it is here that Gould's own ideological preference for progressivism comes through in his highly qualified comment that 'much of the little that is good about modern American education follows an ideal that triumphed with the strong aid of recapitulation' (Gould, 1977, p. 155). That progressivism partly triumphed due to false premises should give us cause for concern and make us question its supposed success as Kieran Egan (2002) points out. He indicates all that is wrong in Spencer, Dewey and Piaget and is a useful corrective to the more descriptive account given in this book.[25]

But we don't have to read his book, just go back to our previous chapter and cognitive load theory. A novice child at the beginning of a task should not be given an open problem to tinker with, eventually solving it through trial and error, because this will result in cognitive overload. We need to build in strong supports and scaffolding at the beginning to reduce extraneous cognitive load and allow enough space for germane cognitive load. Make no mistake, we want a child to reach a level where she is in control of her own learning and actively solving difficult problems, but that's not how you start out. An expert, as Spencer undoubtedly was, would love an open problem to solve, but that is not how a beginner works and we all are beginners again and again in our lives. The danger with allowing an open explorative space for beginners does not only revolve around cognitive overload, but also with time wasting, given the amount we increasingly have to learn in a limited time. Just because our ancestors started in an exploratory mode does not mean that we have to, or should. This is a fallacy. Cognitive load theory clearly points to the need to start off simply and slowly shift to more complex developments; but it certainly does not recommend starting off in the dark when we can provide clear, worked, simple, telling examples that get the learner on the right track. Spencer, it must be said, has a lot for which to answer.

Will the increase in knowledge ever stop and how will education keep up?

What the principle of recapitulation does foreshadow is the issue of the growing amount and complexity of knowledge our modern world is adding cumulatively. This is a version of terminal addition we mentioned earlier, where we have to add more and more on top of an ever-growing pile. The difficulty education has with this growth is compressing all of this information into a manageable set the next generation can master to continue the growth. This is a version of condensation, also mentioned earlier, where more and more has to be compressed into less and less. It is not so much a matter of the individual learner recapitulating what has gone before at the level of humankind, but of the exponential growth in knowledge and what education can do about it. Initially, parental and communal forms of education were sufficient to transfer the knowledge and skill pool from one generation to another, but with the age of enlightenment and industrialisation came the increased production of knowledge, resulting in a gap forming between what communal and folk forms of education could do and the increasing pool of specialised knowledge needed in a modernising world.

Formal schooling arose partly to meet this gap, but this has only resulted in more specialisation and increased knowledge production. Does there not come a time when schools just cannot cope with the amount of new knowledge required to be mastered? And can the same not be said for our children? Will it eventually become impossible for them to learn all that is expected of them? Are we not already finding that we have to cram more and more stuff into our curricula just to keep pace with all the new additions? Many high schools now teach calculus, a mathematics topic that used to be the preserve of universities, and similar pressures are on science, biology, geography, and accounting. This results in compressing more and more stuff earlier and earlier until something has to give. If scientific knowledge is increasing all the time, then surely this flood must spill over into the school curriculum? The seriousness of this pressure becomes more intense when we realise that scientific knowledge is not just growing, it's growing exponentially (figure 5.4). Rather than simple linear growth that adds new elements, the growth is doubling and then doubling again.

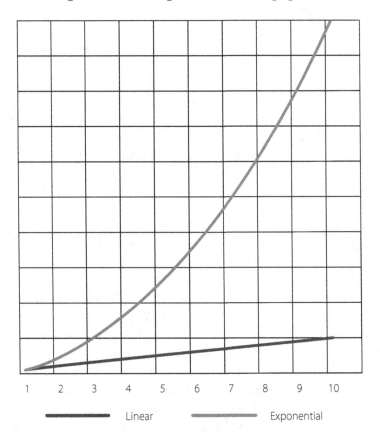

| | | | | | | | | | | |
| 1 | 2 | 3 | 4 | 5 | 6 | 7 | 8 | 9 | 10 |

Linear   Exponential

Figure 5.4 Linear and exponential growth

A good example of this can be seen in the number of mathematics publications that doubles every fifteen years or so. Eventually is there not going to come a point when, like Scotty on Star Trek, we exclaim 'We cannae make it *go 'ny faster!*'

Alex Mesoudi (2011) thinks we shall reach such a saturation point where the exponential accumulation of knowledge has to slow down. Rather than an exponential curve upwards (A) we shall hit a set of real world constraints that will flatten the curve (B).

He points out that the cost of learning the previous generation's accumulated knowledge continually increases as both the amount and complexity of that knowledge grows. It's taking longer and longer to learn.

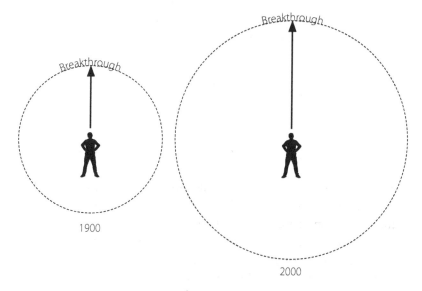

Figure 5.5 Expansion of invention breakthrough point

Mesoudi uses a paper by Jones (2010) to drive the point home. Jones took a look at the mean age at which Nobel Prize winners made their breakthrough discoveries and found it was going up. The same trend was found with significant inventors. In 1900 the breakthroughs tended to happen at around the age of 32; by 2000 it had gone up to 38. A longer period of training and mastery is needed. If we put a scientist as a baby in the middle of a circle that represents all s/he needs to master in order to get to the point where a new breakthrough is possible, represented by reaching the circumference of a circle, then in 1900 the scientist had less distance to travel than in 2000 (figure 5.5).

Even though it's taking longer for scientists to reach mastery levels that enable breakthrough, there is no corresponding increase in productivity over the age of 40. We still age in the same way. The reason why there is more knowledge being continually added has to do with the growing population of scientists, not that individual scientists are producing more in old age (with exceptions, of course.)

In 2000 scientists are taking longer to get to the point where breakthroughs are made, but still showing the same drop off in productivity after hitting 40, probably due to assorted family commitments and mid-life crises (figure 5.6).

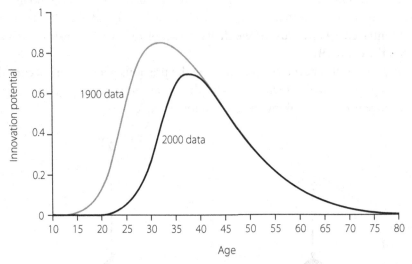

Figure 5.6 Comparison of breakthrough point in 1900 and 2000

Scientists have responded in part to this dilemma by intensifying the focus of their specialisation, thus reducing the amount of content and time needed before breakthrough becomes possible. But this results in such narrowing that it becomes difficult to see the bigger picture and get a sense of the possible applications of the research, and a drop in innovation potential. Another trick used by scientists is to take drugs that concentrate the mind, the only problem being that this enables intense focus on details whilst disenabling emergence of the big picture.

In chapter 3 we explored how to increase the capacity of our working memories, even though it stays limited to around four slots, by chunking, long-term memory networks and automaticity. Is it possible to do the same at the level of our species when we are faced with a tidal wave of knowledge threatening our future ability to innovate? Can we improve the way we educate to the point where we keep abreast of the increasing amount and complexity of knowledge? Can we condense and compact what needs to be learnt while at the same time working out the most effective ways to teach what is most important in the first thirty years of an individual's educational history? Or should we search for another way of living life on this planet and doing this thing called education? The worrying aspect about the above discussion is that improvements in education will probably only delay saturation point, not get rid of it. Maybe some kind of levelling off is what is needed. If Z in figure 5.7 simply represents the amount of knowledge and t the amount of time used for education, and assuming we can go from our current efficiencies in education (B) to a more supercharged education (C), are we not simply delaying the inevitable at massive cost to our children who will start education at three and graduate at thirty, working all day and studying every night simply to get to a point where something interesting can be said? Japanese children are already feeling the pressure. Their evenings, weekends and holidays are all sacrificed in the struggle to master the ever-growing pile of knowledge. Is there a limit, where no matter how efficient education is, and no matter how hard students learn, there comes a point where we just cannot learn any more in a lifetime, where the upward curve of learning new knowledge has to flatten out, as indicated by the supercharged education line below? Or given our ability to chunk information into bigger and more cohesive systems, and our ability to condense more and more information into tighter and tighter networks, can we not keep moving learning upwards and outwards?

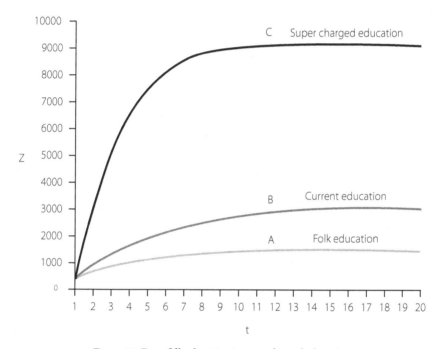

Figure 5.7 From folk education to supercharged education

So what are the educational moves being made at species level to improve the amount and complexity of what we learn and how we learn it? Well, first we are spending more and more time learning. And this is not only in the Far East. My friends' daughter, who is currently (2015) ten years old, finishes her day on average at six at night, sometimes later, because of all the things she has to learn and practise. And then she still has to do homework.

One way to escape this massive expansion in the time needed for learning is to make a grand plan of what is needed to be learned and then stick to it, day by day. Take the fundamental and intermediate levels of all the organised knowledge of humanity and make maps of it that go from simple to complex in various subjects, as Spencer suggested. Then organise lessons or modules for each element as well as the links you need either to go forward into more complexity, backwards to simpler elements, or across into similar and related areas. Again, this is much as Spencer envisioned in his account of the progression of science. Start with basic elements, simple links and clear levels that build up into higher and higher levels. Spencer suggests that these will tend to be subjects that have worked out how to quantify their focus area in systematic and formalised ways. Make sure that every module provides enough opportunity for practice and experimentation (Spencer's fourth principle, but make sure that this is done in ways that work carefully with cognitive load by scaffolding the process), with assessments that check whether the student has grasped the main point, and ensure the particulars build towards a greater whole.

Once the student has successfully completed a module, open out possible future modules based on past performance, type of interest, similar themes and, most important, use modules that are one level of complexity higher. Make this map of knowledge and all its lessons freely available for anyone to use at any time in any way they want, but order it so that there is a logical progression (Spencer's fifth principle). Expect that, given this room to work in your own time and pace with discoveries set to build up cumulatively, there will be an explosion of energy and excitement that motivate and drive students (Spencer's sixth principle); and that by navigating their own path they will trace the fundamentals of our current knowledge base. Every person in the world will have access to all knowledge in a structured and principled form and be able to chart a path through it that leads from simple to complex, from concrete to abstract, from the empirical to the rational, across different subjects, each subject moving off from a simple and basic starting point and going in individuated directions that often resonate and integrate at higher levels with each other. And what's more, if you really like the idea, then go onto the Internet now and take a look at how this route is currently being chased, in a very early and still developing form, by Salman Khan.

From one class schoolroom to one world classroom

Salman Khan was a hedge fund analyst settling in to his million dollar a year salary. In 2004 he posted some maths lessons on YouTube for his cousins. As he sardonically notes in his excellent Technology, Entertainment, Design (TED) talk, they preferred the Internet version because they could pause and repeat him at their leisure. They could use a very public medium for their own personalised learning. What Khan did not expect was the uptake from various other YouTubers who could do the same thing. Excited comments started to accumulate from people suddenly understanding concepts they had not been able to grasp before, and doing it in their own space and time at their own pace. For Khan, the hedge fund analyst, this was a good feeling; to be doing something of social rather than monetary value. And what was more, each of the lessons he posted on YouTube stayed there to be used by as anyone who had access to the Internet. Unlike other people who posted lessons on the Internet, Khan kept going. He currently (2015) has over five thousand videos of himself teaching individual modules that have been delivered from YouTube over 500 million times. This kind of response has generated enormous interest and funding, enabling Khan to take the videos way beyond a set of extra lessons for his cousins. It's taken him to a point where he can start to taste what it would mean to have a global, one world classroom offering high quality education for anyone at any time: a free virtual school for the world (Khan, 2012). At the beginning of 2015 he has 15 million students in 190 countries. Obviously there are massive fall out rates and YouTube views that don't last for longer than a couple of seconds, but this does not counter the fact that millions of students are learning maths, science, biology, computer programming, and many other subjects through this world portal to education.

Khan has the beginnings of a foundational map of the formalised knowledge of humanity. It's at a very early stage, but its working principles have already emerged. It works from simple to complex; and from a generic skill set, it differentiates into individuated subjects that use the same base but go in different directions. Each module comes with an extensive set of exercises (that provide immediate feedback) and once you get the ten questions right, you move on to more advanced modules. You go from pre-algebra to early algebra to algebra to pre-calculus, and also have the choice to move into different fields of knowledge like logic, computer programming, grammar and genetics. Most of these fields are quantifiable and have explicit combinatorial rules that build on each other, allowing for a hierarchical organisation that shifts into an increasingly networked set of links as you reach higher levels, which often demand a number of lower-level modules from different areas.

To encourage interest and continued participation Khan has used numerous strategies. Immediate and continuous feedback is generated through an enormous bank of tests that provide the student with guidance and correction. Encouragement is given through a system of rewards and 'games' (badges, avatars, points, missions) that provide extra impetus and energy. Even an old gnarly professor like me gets happy when he gets a badge after doing a particularly hard section on fractions.

Schoolteachers have picked up these video lessons. Initially just the videos were shown in class, but with the design of practice exercises a whole new world opened out. Imagine a device that tracked what every single learner was doing in the lesson, plus all previous lessons, using the videos and responses recorded on a tablet. A teacher could see where every learner was, where they were doing well and where they were struggling, what their choices and patterns of learning were, and how fast or slowly they were moving through sections. Rather than giving a one-size-fits-all lesson, the teacher is freed to move around the class helping individual learners, armed with data that shows where excellence and problems lie. Imagine all this data going into massive data banks to be analysed for possible improvements and eliminations of inefficiencies.

Homework can become a very different phenomenon with this kind of pedagogy. You go home to do the actual lessons in your own time and come to school to discuss them and check on your questions, misunderstandings, confusions and suggestions. The classroom flips, with school done at home and revision at school. Khan calls this the flipped classroom.

Some anecdotal evidence is emerging from tracking students. There are often sections that individual learners take a long time to master and then there is a burst of speed where a number of modules are quickly completed before another module is hit that takes longer. These vary per individual, but it does not matter as each individual can work at their own pace.

More than this, the teacher could keep track of the class as a whole.

Khan has developed a dashboard system that keeps track of the whole class, with both individual trajectories and overall performance updated in real time as the students go through the course. The dashboard does not only work in classrooms. Parents could use it for individual children; districts for the relative performance of schools; countries to keep track of all their students; and the world to account for its own learning. Tau, floating above us, could keep track of how we are doing relative to other intelligent life forms.

This is a little too much to ask of one person who has currently (2015) recorded almost 5000 YouTube videos, even if he intends to continue posting videos for the rest of his life (which he does.) It's also too much for video technology, which on its own cannot replace all the other forms of education out there, or all the ways pedagogic interactions happen. Sal Khan does not make this claim and indeed he hopes that the videos will, if anything, free up teacher time precisely to pursue more complex and dynamic pedagogic practices. But what Khan is coming to appreciate, as the millions of hits on his videos grow, is that there are teachers out there who have done what he has done in ways that are better than his own intuitive approach, struggled with ways of improving comprehension of a concept by interrogating the minutiae, and developed ways of teaching that result in deep understanding and mastery rather than a superficial sense of having grasped a concept by answering ten questions. This has even forced Khan to remove videos that contain mistakes, meanderings or badly put sections. What he is doing intuitively has often been done by others in more pedagogically rewarding modes, with better structuring of earlier learning, more profound assessments and more rigorous pushing forward to higher levels of complexity or more intense levels of application. Sal, as he likes to be called, currently (2015) has a team of eighty people. As the Khan website proudly puts it:

What started as one man tutoring his cousin has grown into an 80-person organization. We're a diverse team that has come together to work on an audacious mission: to provide a free world-class education for anyone, anywhere. We are developers, teachers, designers, strategists, scientists, and content specialists who passionately believe in inspiring the world to learn.[26]

What he has done enables us to glimpse what it would mean to have a one-world classroom that would open out for all of us the ever-growing knowledge of humanity in ways that take us beyond formal schooling as we currently experience it.

Chapter 6

From one-world classroom to one learning sequence

Making all the knowledge of the world pedagogically available in an organised and accessible form for everyone, anywhere, any time is a twenty-first century project, but this vision is built on the success of each elementary learning sequence and how they combine. And it is in these details that the devil lies. Khan cannot do it on his own, no matter how many lessons he posts and organises on his knowledge map; that is why he has eighty highly qualified, dynamic workers helping out. But as astonishing as Khan Academy is, we already have hundreds of thousands of good textbooks and thousands of curriculum plans mapping out both the content and sequences of hundreds of subjects across hundreds of countries, never mind the individualised lesson scripts of millions of teachers going out to billions of students continuously as the world quietly rotates on its axis. What strategies are possible on a micro level and can these micro-elements somehow organise and cohere into a supercharged education environment that pushes beyond our rapidly aging formalised schooling model? So just as we shifted from the macro picture of all the schools of the world to a micro focus on desks, chairs, and writing equipment; we now shift from the macro perspective of all the world's knowledge to a micro focus on learning sequences. Four recent developments give us clues to the shape of the new terrain of education: ontology-based learning path generation schemes, learning hierarchies, lesson objects and free access learning.

The problem with Khan's virtual school of the world is that his video lessons cannot change and adapt to the specific requirements of the student. The lessons can reach any student who has access to the Internet and the determination to self-direct learning. The student can stop and start, rewind and go forward at her own pace, but the lesson itself cannot change its starting point, sequence and end point. Khan would have to redo the video lesson, which he does, but he still has thousands of future lessons to do, making looking backwards very difficult indeed. With many of his lessons he has already done them twice after working out misunderstandings; but a third rework and a fourth?

If you step out of Khan's self-contained virtual classroom into the chaotic environment of available lessons online, which lessons are better than others and how do they combine? You can find whatever you want, but often under conditions of cognitive overload and wastage. Individual teachers can organise this chaos and adapt sequences for their own students, but they are tied to one place, one time and one batch of students. Is it possible to develop an automatic learning sequence that starts where an individual learner needs it to start, moves in a sequence that adapts to the responses of the student, and from performance assessment develops better learning sequences and so on in a virtuous circle of continuous pedagogic improvement? Let's get clear what possibility this question is pointing to – a system that automatically improves its ability to respond to individuals based on their particular demands and abilities. Any student, at any level, can start at any point, and the computer program will work out where the student is and what to do next that is in tune with the student. At a micro level you would need the following ingredients: a learning task that involves a number of steps; a possible set of sequences through the learning task ordered in different ways; a pre-test that identifies prior knowledge; a post-test that evaluates the results and effectiveness of the learning sequence; and a way of re-ordering or changing the sequences based on student responses to the pre-test, during the sequence and afterwards so as to develop optimal learning pathways. If this worked, then a virtual school of the world could have inbuilt evolutionary mechanisms for the improvement of each of its lessons. The more the lessons were used, the better they would get because the mechanism would work out the best sequences of learning for individual students based on personal past history and the responses of all other students. You would go online, do a pre-test, from which the programme will work out what level you start on, and then based on your responses as you go through the lesson, it would change and adapt the lesson steps to suit your own peculiar demands, strengths and deficiencies, based on the results of thousands of responses and effects before you. Artificial intelligence combined with mass use becomes a pedagogic tool to improve our individual intelligence radically.

Pedagogic engineering

Chih-Ming Chen (2009) provides a glimpse of how this is possible using ontology-based concept maps to develop personalised learning paths. (I can't help but perversely chuckle as I write this: after dutifully going through ontogeny recapitulating phylogeny you get thrown into ontology-based concept maps.)

Ontology, in information science and artificial intelligence technologies, is something different from its meaning in philosophy (Smart, 2003), but there is a general overlap where both are concerned with what exists and how to sort it into different categories. Both work with kinds of objects and processes, how they are structured and how they relate. Ontology refers to what the object is and what its elements are. Within the computer-based learning community, ontology refers to a defined vocabulary of all the relevant terms in a subject area as well as their logical relations and combinations.

Ontology dreams of providing a complete classification of everything that exists and provides the fraught beginnings of a technical armoury needed to tackle the question of how to organise pedagogically all the knowledge of the world. I say fraught because both in the information sciences and philosophy, the task of developing a classification of the world has turned out to be massively complex and contested. Classification schemes conflict and hive off in different directions, depending on focus and purpose. Using a concept from the previous chapter we could say they individuate in different directions, making a general ontology of all subjects an almost impossible task or one that is doomed to stay at such a generic level it says nothing of value to individuated disciplines. Another problem is that certain types of knowledge are better suited to a strictly defined vocabulary and a small set of logical relations. It doesn't work that well on Shakespeare, for example. Furthermore, pedagogic undertakings involve far more than working out a classification scheme. It is necessary to select from the classification what is needed in real time in a specific context, elaborate on it, sequence it, and evaluate it in its transformed state. But that does not mean ontology should be relegated to the background in the twenty-first century project to make all knowledge available to anyone at any time in any place in pedagogically enlightening ways that automatically configure to individual profiles. It means that ontology sits as a troubled necessity of our modern educational project.

If ontology is about how to carve the world up at its joints, what is an ontology-based concept map? It's an attempt to take a specific domain of knowledge and provide clear definitions of the basic concepts and processes attached to it, as well as how they combine and interact. Let's take a simple, well-defined domain like 'fractions' as a starting point. Two immediate problems jump out: what are the basic concepts and operations needed to understand how fractions work; and how do they relate to each other? Even if you were able to gain some clarity on the elements, the problem is that some are more basic than others and some need other elements as building blocks. Let's say you identified seventeen different elementary units needed to understand fractions by consulting expert teachers and textbooks. You would still need to work out the order in which they should be placed. This would not be arbitrary. You could not do them in any random order: some sequences would be better than others; but which ones and for whom? If you asked expert teachers or consulted textbooks you would find that even after reaching agreement on the basic units, there would be different sequential orderings. At this point Chen does something very interesting. He administers a fraction test based on the seventeen units to six hundred elementary learners and then ranks the units according to difficulty based on wrong answers (the more learners get the unit wrong, the harder it is.) This gave him a ranking order from 1 to 17 based on the difficulty level of the course material (Chen, 2009, p. 1035), with 1 being easiest and 17 hardest.

1 – Equal parts
2 – Division as sharing
3 – Division as separating
4 – Sharing with a remainder
5 – Separating with a remainder
6 – Parts of a whole
7 – Improper fractions
8 – Sequence of fractions
9 – Comparing proper fractions with the same denominator
10 – Comparing proper fractions with different denominators
11 – Adding and subtracting fractions
12 – Adding fractions
13 – Subtracting fractions
14 – Missing addend
15 – Missing subtrahend
16 – Missing summand
17 – Missing minuend

Using this as a sequencing base, he compared it to the way four Taiwanese textbooks ordered the seventeen components and what he found is fascinating, if unsurprising. Each of the textbooks orders the seventeen units into different sequences. The *teaching* order did not necessarily follow the *difficulty* order (Chen, 2009, p. 1046).

What you could do at this point is just average out the teaching orders of the four textbooks and work with the most common combinations as your integrated teaching sequence, but this is dangerous as there are reasons behind each textbook sequence that put them on different paths. If at an early point in the sequence you choose to go with one option rather than another, this powerfully impacts on how the rest of the sequence unfolds. Averaging it out could create a mush in which different functioning paths are melted into one fuzzy mess. Even more complicating, all the textbooks put some fairly easy components near the end, because, even though they were easy, they were only needed once the basic steps of working with fractions had been worked on. Number 7, for example (improper fractions), is only of middling difficulty but it comes near the end of all the textbook sequences. This helps provide some clues to ordering the sequence of units that goes beyond just using level of difficulty. What matters is the *internal logic of the sequence*, not only moving from simple to difficult. A further complication arises from how different learners perform in the pre-test. They make different kinds of mistakes in different units and the units they can and cannot do are different from other learners. It's not as simple as designing a sequence that works from one to seventeen and placing learners somewhere on the sequence. It's about working out what kinds of combination to offer individual learners based on their previous knowledge base. Each learner will show a different profile depicting what they can and cannot do and the difficulty is working out which sequence to offer them in response to their profile. Expert teachers can do this, and that is why they are so valuable; but can a computer programme?

Chen tries to show how it is possible by quantifying the relationships between the conceptual units. Unlike an expert teacher, who qualitatively understands how fractions work as a whole and the different paths through the whole course, a computer can only work with quantification and decision trees based on it. If the quantification process works, then rather than have an expert teacher always on hand to decide which way to go with different learners, the learning sequence becomes automated but still provides individual learning paths that work. Chen attempts to do this by taking the test records of the six hundred elementary school students who did the fraction test and looks for correlation frequencies between the incorrect and correct answers. He puts them into a concept correlation table in which the higher the number the stronger the correlation. It allows him to work out which concepts are related to which based on what learners can and cannot do. It basically quantifies the following logic: if the learner can do this and this, then they also tend to be able to do that and that; if the learner cannot do this and this, then they tend not to be able to do that and that; and just because learners can do this unit does not mean they can do that unit, and so on. It starts to match the same qualitative process of an expert teacher, but does it blindly according to numbers (Chen, 2009, p. 1038).

You don't get sequences from a correlation table, but clusters where different concept units hang together with high frequencies. Chen finds ten clusters. Forgive me for not getting into the precise mechanics of how he does this as there is a more general point I want to illustrate. The point is that he is able to combine the levels of difficulty of the seventeen units with a conceptual ordering into ten clusters and it is this combination that gives him an ontology-based concept map (Chen, 2009, p. 1040) that works with both increasing difficulty and how the different components of fractions hang together in clusters. Get something wrong in one cluster and the computer knows what other elements you probably don't understand, and can take you there automatically.

One final point on this strange new world of pedagogic engineering. The textbook analysis of all the different sequences revealed that number 10 (comparing fractions with different denominators) always came right at the end. This component was not the most difficult at all, but it does contain within its operations the basic elements of all the other components. All the clusters correlate highly with component 10. Component 10 might not be the hardest element, but it's the one that all the others refer to and in all the textbook sequences it comes right at the end because it contains elements of all the others.

It's still very early days for this kind of intricate pedagogic engineering, but it is certainly not the last we shall hear of this kind of work. Big education companies like Pearson are charging ahead with these kinds of programming technologies because they offer cheap and automated alternatives to expensive teachers but still offer individualised feedback. Eventually this sort of programming starts to feed off its own base. It keeps track of learner performance before, during and after the module has been worked through. It can blindly work out which sequences work for what kind of student profile and continuously improve the way it does this by checking the success of the sequence selection in the post-test. Over time the best sequences for all sorts of learner profiles will emerge, making it a formidable competitor to the expert teacher. Imagine a virtual classroom of the world that takes you from where you are and plots a learning course especially for you based on what thousands of other students have found works, or does not work, for them; all done automatically. For capitalists in education it offers massive profits at minimal cost.

I have a complex reaction to this kind of pedagogic engineering. On the one hand it sets up a solution to the problem of cognitive overload and wasted time that comes with the explosion of information on the Web and the proliferation of e-learning sites. Learners become disoriented by the choices available and disheartened by dead end paths that don't link up into a more systematic and coherent whole or by going through a predetermined sequence that does not fit their own knowledge profile. Automated conceptual ontology maps offer a vision of a world classroom that uniquely adapts itself to each learner and continually improves how it does this as more and more students use it. On the other hand, it sets up the conceptual sequences based on external and quantitative drivers such as levels of difficulty and the clustering of mistaken answers to tests, not on the actual internal logic of the subject. Out of the ordering of fractions in the four Taiwanese textbooks, is there not a way to decide which are optimal, based on how fractions work? What about locking the four writers of the textbooks up in a room and telling them they can only come out once they have agreed on the best sequences? Note I am not saying one best sequence, that is a simple-minded dream we have to throw away. There will always be a number of paths to the same end point, but we should not forget that a good teacher uses the internal logic of the subject, not external quantifications, to work them out. But with quantification comes the possibility of breaking away from dependence on one teacher at one time in one place, and reaching for a world that can adapt to any student at any time in any place. The specialised work of teaching is in the process of becoming an algorithm. Just as pharmacists are being replaced with diagnostic software that asks you ten questions and then prescribes your medicine, so too are teachers being replaced with pedagogic software that asks you ten questions and then prescribes a learning sequence.

Learning hierarchies and cumulative learning

Structuring a learning sequence qualitatively, based on the internal logic of a specific topic, concept or capability, has a long and venerable history in instructional design. One of the earliest and clearest articulations of how to do it comes from Gagné's work (1962) on learning hierarchies (Richey, 2000). At the heart of the process lies the asking of the same question over and over again of a specific task or topic, each time at a lower and more specific level: 'What would the individual already have to know how to do in order to learn this new capability simply by being given verbal instructions?' (Richey, 2000, p. 68).

Notice that this question does not deal specifically with the content of the topic, but with the subordinate skills. It's a hierarchy of capabilities, not of concepts. Notice as well that the question has a peculiar edge to it: what sub-components must a student know in order suddenly, at a certain point, to find that she can handle the new capability simply by being asked to do it. It is kind of what happens with the fraction example above, C10: compare proper fractions with different denominators. When asking this question on the addition of integers, figure 6.1 is what Gagné came up with (Richey, 2000, p. 65).

Pre-tests were then designed for students to check which subordinate tasks they could and could not do. Each student was then taught how to do the subordinate tasks they could not do, starting at the lower levels and moving upwards. Once the teaching was done and all students could do all the subordinate tasks, each student was simply given the verbal instruction to complete the task; and – surprise, surprise – almost all of them could.

Why did Gagné call this process a learning hierarchy? Intuitively the answer is a simple one: because you can only do a higher skill once you have mastered a lower skill on which the higher skill depends. And this is precisely what was shown. Students who could do subordinate skill I in figure 6.1 could do all the other skills underneath. Students who could not do skill I, but could manage subordinate skill II could do subordinate skills III, IV and V. There were no students who could somehow do task I and tasks II, but not V (a, b), IV (a, b) or III (a, b) and II (a, b). The relationship between the subordinate skills is asymmetrical. It works in one direction, but not in the other and goes from simple to complex. It starts with simple responses and builds up into chains of responses, which enable multiple discriminations that build into concepts. These are combined into simple rules and they are then combined into more complex rules. You can only get to the complex set of rules once you understand the simpler concepts and rules of which it is made.

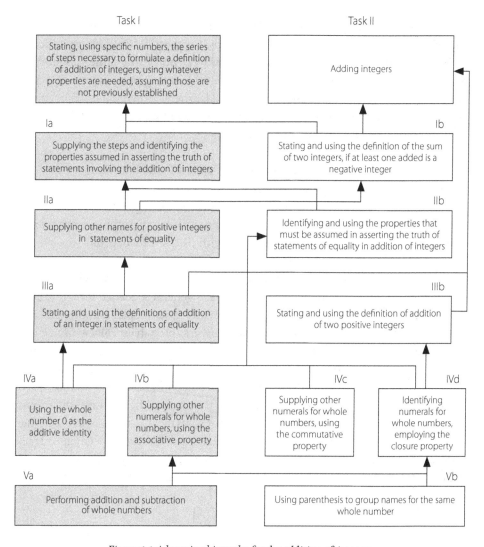

Figure 6.1 A learning hierarchy for the addition of integers

This is a different way of working out levels of difficulty from that of Chen's strategy of ranking items based on the amount of learner error in tests: it works with a logical hierarchical skill structure rather than emergent patterns based on learner responses. In no way does this mean that the hierarchical analysis is always correct. What is needed after an initial breakdown analysis are empirical try outs that test where the skill is located in the hierarchy: 'whether a particular skill transfers positively to another, or whether they are independent, or whether perhaps they co-vary in their transfer effects'. Gagné notes that his own work on this is primitive: 'I perceive these to be very unsophisticated compared with procedures I can only dimly imagine' (Richey, 2000, p. 69).

One can only imagine what he would have made of artificial intelligence combining with ontology-based concept maps. I suspect he would have critically embraced some of the developments. Gagné was not a one-dimensional man who insisted on a rigid following of hierarchical learning programmes. He was clear that there is no one exclusive route for all learners. Individual learners might skip some of the subordinate tasks or use knowledge from a different domain to help complete the task in a different way:

> A learning hierarchy, then, in the present state of our knowledge, cannot represent a unique or most efficient route for any given learner. Instead, what it represents is the most probable expectation of greatest positive transfer for an entire sample of learners concerning whom we know nothing more than what specifically relevant skills they start with (Richey, 2000, p. 69).

Chen and Gagné start in very different places: Chen with an emergent logic of difficulty based on error count and Gagné with a general sequence for cumulative learning that works downwards from complex rules to its simpler components. But both wish to develop a learning programme that works probabilistically with an entire set of learners and both use the responses of the learners to inform developments.

Gagné points to three surprising moves individuals could make that break with an expected hierarchical learning pattern: they might jump a level; transfer knowledge or skill from another domain that helps them move differently through the levels; or combine elements in an atypical way to reach a higher level (figure 6.2). He did not have the computational resources of Chen to track individual responses and build them into a larger optional sequential set through probabilistic equations, but he could 'dimly imagine them' (Richey, 2000, p. 71).

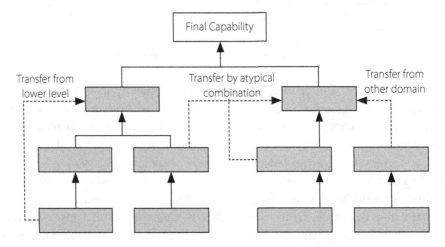

Figure 6.2 The latent consequences of cumulative learning

Gagné was brilliant, but why did he insist that learning hierarchies should deal with intellectual skills and strategies, not the content and concepts of the task? He wanted a final capability (figure 6.2), not understanding of higher concepts. I have learned to be critically respectful with founding fathers as it is often their first visions that are the clearest. However, I have an allergic reaction to skills talk, especially of the supposedly universal or generic kind. I take it to be one of the major blights of our current educational landscape because it mostly destroys detailed engagement with knowledge structures and exchanges it for an empty set of generic skills. But on this point Gagné is unrelenting: '[ask] what the individual can do ... and avoid ... what the individual knows' (Richey, 2000, p. 71).

It was not concepts he wanted to put in a learning hierarchy, but intellectual skills. Rather than the elementary building blocks of a learning hierarchy, Gagné wanted to get at its sub-routines – its sub-methods, sub-procedures, and sub-steps – at the compositional logics of the larger final capability. Gagné did not want the variable content that gets used by the sub-routines to be the focus of learning hierarchies as this would be mistaking the content structure for the hierarchical driver.

This was not because he did not see the importance of stored, verbalisable knowledge. You need to have a basic vocabulary of concepts otherwise the intellectual skill will not hold in specific instances. Intellectual skill without content is not only empty, it's often worthless. However, intellectual skills 'have an ordered relation to each other such that subordinate ones contribute positive transfer to superordinate ones' (Richey, 2000, p. 74), whereas verbalisable entities do not necessarily have this relationship to each other. Intellectual skills go from simple to complex, whereas verbalisable entities can be learned in all sorts of different orders and ways. It's where skills build on each other that you have both positive transfer from simple to complex capabilities and cumulative learning that builds continuously upwards. If you get a learning hierarchy right, then learners who achieve a correctly developed set of subordinate skills radically increase their chances of being able to do the superordinate skill. It's almost a learning fairy tale where what seemed impossible to do as a final capability comes naturally after all the steps have been worked through. You will always need to add to learning hierarchies the content and concepts needed for specific understanding and practice, but what drives positive transfer is the proper non-symmetrical ordering of intellectual skills from simple to complex. Completed correctly, when the learner is given the finishing verbal instruction to demonstrate the final capability, She finds she already knows everything she needs; and she just does it.

Gagné was clear that the ordering of a learning hierarchy from simple intellectual skill to complex intellectual skills did not have to determine directly the ordering of the actual learning process in real time (Richey, 2000, p. 75). The presentation sequence could be different from the learning hierarchy. This is not just because learners do surprising things (like jump levels, make idiosyncratic links and bring in insights from other domains), but because intellectual skills are not the only things learners do. They have to learn verbal information like concepts and terms; cognitive strategies that assist in the self-management of learning; smooth and errorless performance of motor skills; and attitudes that help drive actions in positive ways. None of these other learning outcomes work in strictly hierarchic ways. Verbal information tends to be learned best when presented in an organised, meaningful context; cognitive strategies are learned as students encounter different situations that demand self-regulation at different times, depending on the problem at hand; motor skills need continual and repetitive practice; and attitudes come from interacting with human beings who act as role models. Different learning outcomes need different types of instruction to be effective.

Is it possible to work out an efficient sequence of instruction that holds across these different learning outcomes? Such a sequence would hold enormous value for the project to make all the knowledge of the world pedagogically available to everyone because it would provide, on top of a conceptual ontology or learning hierarchy, a way to pedagogically sequence a lesson from beginning to end that all teachers could use. Where would we look for clues to find such a strange creature? Gagné suggests that we first turn to the internal processes of how we learn and, in 1970's terms, gives an account of working and long-term memory, executive control, and reinforcement that harmonises well with our own account in chapter 4.

> Following reception of incoming stimuli, information is registered very briefly in one or more sensory registers, then undergoes feature analysis or selective perception. The information next enters short-term memory where it can be stored in limited amounts for only about 20 seconds. Here it may be rehearsed and is also subject to semantic encoding, in which form it enters the long-term memory. Information from long-term memory may be retrieved back to a short- term form, which is in this case viewed as working memory. Working memory (conscious memory) is where various combinations of new and old information take place ... Executive control [is] a means by which the learner exerts control over the other processes of learning and memory ... [R]einforcement takes place ... [where] the after-effects of successful performance have their well-known effects on subsequent performances (Richey, 2000, pp. 113–114).

If this is how the internal process of learning works, then surely an external sequence of instructional events could support and influence it. How would this external sequence of instruction work?

First, the attention of the student is drawn to the topic (1) and the learner is informed of the objective for the lesson (2). Prior learning is recalled and activated

(3) before the distinctive new elements are demonstrated (4) and the learner engages in the process of learning the new material in an organised way (5). The learner then tries to show, in some kind of way, that she can actually do what has been learned (6) and informative feedback is given (7) before a final assessment of the performance is undertaken (8) and further practice and applications given to integrate the skill into existing practices (9). This element of further practice is crucial as it results in automisation of basic skills and releases attention to focus on the development of higher level thinking processes.

Not all of this sequence of instructional events has to happen explicitly in every lesson as often elements occur implicitly in the flow. And some of the events happen very differently, depending on whether the learning outcome is working with a motor skill, attitude, intellectual skill, verbal knowledge, executive function, or some combination of them. But it still provides a way of setting up the external flow of a lesson in a way that works with our internal processes of learning.

Lessons do not happen in isolation: they combine in larger goals or whole tasks, and these consist of numerous objectives that mix with each other, often involving a combination of verbal knowledge, intellectual skill, executive control, attitude and motor skill. It means that an instructional designer cannot simply rest with the intricate details of a learning task, but has to look at the larger goal behind the various elements and then work out how to hold them all together. Gagné only dealt with this late in his intellectual career (in collaboration with Merrill in 1990) when the necessity of a structuring frame was recognised. Learners would need a frame or schema for the underlying purpose behind a number of lessons to hold. This frame would help them work out when and how different skills and knowledge are needed in pursuit of a more integrated set of goals in a larger enterprise. Gagné was not able to take this forward as he died in 2002, but this question of how to combine various learning objects into a larger whole task framework continues to puzzle. Two very different answers have been proposed in the last twenty years. The first is a radically egalitarian model that pushes for each small learning object to stand on its own feet, independent and free, enabled to combine and intersect with whatever other learning objects happen to resonate with it. The second is a more structured model that proposes a whole task framework holding all the elements together in a co-ordinated pedagogic sequence.

Learning objects

The atomistic idea of independent objects freely interacting with each other depending on the case at hand has been around since Democritus, but its current learning object digital form was mooted in 1992. Imagine a teaching scenario where you have a whole course to put together, but do not want to waste time reinventing the wheel when other teachers have already done many of the elements in interesting, creative and pedagogically insightful ways. At what point (if any) in the imaginary scenario sketched below would you start to feel uncomfortable?

Your first option is to go on the Web and find raw media objects (songs, sound bites, illustrations, diagrams and text) and stitch them into your course. On the one hand this is the simplest of activities: you search the topic, find an interesting example and use it in your own lesson. These raw media objects are the easiest of elements to re-use in different contexts. But you will also find other teachers have taken these raw objects and used them to illustrate the same concept or process in which you are interested. Let's call this an information object. They save you time as they have already worked the raw media object into a basic pedagogic unit that you can use, rather than having to do the pedagogic work yourself. It might be an introduction, a concept, a principle, a demonstration, an activity, or a summary within the topic. These information objects can be pulled together to deal with a specific learning outcome or objective, and this would give you a learning object. Learning objects are still specific enough to be re-usable across contexts because they deal with a definable outcome. A teacher could at this point use learning objects as a part of her lessons and benefit from the collegial work of her peers who have put these learning objects on the Web for re-use. A Salman Khan video on adding fractions, for example, could be used as part of a lesson. A number of these learning objects could now be stitched together as a full lesson object: the whole lesson consists of different learning objects put together in a useful order. These lesson objects could be combined with other lesson objects and then used as a full course object over a term.

As a classroom teacher I start to feel uncomfortable at around the learning object level. Anything larger than this feels as if the teacher is being somehow irresponsible and unfair to her learners. Behind the sense of irresponsibility lies the failure of the teacher to adapt the lesson to the contextual demands of the class. Learning objects can still be used in adjustable ways within a lesson, but a whole lesson object would probably run roughshod over the particular demands of the learners and the school. A whole lesson is too large and context-bound a unit to be plonked into any classroom in the world, unless it was part of a bigger course that was designed from beginning to end. At the learning object level there is still freedom to move and adapt, and a teacher can use the learning object in fruitful and interesting ways. At a lesson level this freedom disappears. It also becomes exceptionally difficult to combine different lesson objects from across the Web into a course object. Each lesson on the Web would have its own starting and end points, its own developing logics, its own assumptions about what has gone prior and is coming after. The only way out of this problem is either to accept that the unabridged course needs to be designed from the bottom up and presented as a whole on the Web; or that learning objects are the largest one can go if you desire a mix and match world of pedagogy

There is a lot of money to be made from either learning objects or whole courses. Websites are now up and running where teachers can sell their learning objects to other teachers. Teacherspayteachers.com is one such site, where resources as small as an information object and as large as a course object can be bought and sold. The objects are classified into resource types: lesson plans, activities, quizzes, worksheets, white board activities, power points, novel studies, and so on (the resource type list has over a hundred categories.) Each object is cheap to buy, but teachers make money from the number sold with successful teacher designers making small fortunes. At the larger learning object level, there are objects such as 'learning /ar/ with Pirate Mark (r-controlled vowels)' that consists of a 38-page set of lesson plans and activities, comprising a Pirate Mark book (pp. 3–9), Pirate Mark sentence strip cut-outs (pp. 9–16), a recording sheet for listening activity (p. 17), Pirate Mark single page poem (p. 18), literacy centre game (pp. 19–22), art project templates (pp. 23–26), whole group treasure hunt activity (pp. 27–30), Pirate mark /ar/reminder picture (p. 31), sample lesson plan (p. 32), and so on.[27] It costs $5. The seller's nickname is Babbling Abbey. She had 9 257 followers on 7 November 2012, 791 votes (all glowing with comments like 'arghh! This is a treasure') and a number of other products for sale. What makes the site work so well is the way it categorises the learning objects by grade level, subject, resource type and price as well as a number of other categories. Each resource has a metadata description that defines the object on a number of levels and depending on your search criteria it either gets thrown up for you to peruse or not.

The reason why I chose 'learning /ar/with Pirate Mark' is that although it is a large learning object, it is not a course. It focuses on one skill (ar) rather than a whole reading programme and can be broken up and used in all sorts of different ways. Planning a whole course over an extended period is a very different endeavour. It was at this point that Gagné ended his career without being able to take it further. One learning outcome is hard enough to design for: what of a complex task or competence that takes months or years to master and involves numerous skills and concepts that combine and intersect in all sorts of different ways? How would you make this available for anyone to access any time and be automatically responsive to the student?

How one of the most exclusive universities in the world managed to become one of the most open

Massachusetts Institute of Technology (MIT) took a bold step forward in answering this question by freely making available its courses on the Web. As of the middle of 2014 it has over 2 000 courses visited by close to a 100 million visitors (http://ocw.mit.edu/about/site-statistics/monthly-reports/MITOCW_DB_2014_03.pdf). You can go to many of them and start immediately. I chose

Foundations of Biology (Eric Lander, Robert Weinberg, Tyler Jacks, Hazel Sive, Graham Walker, Sallie Chisholm and Michelle Mischke) as it is one of the most recent courses on the site designed for independent study.[28] It is not simply a set of lectures recorded on video and uploaded to the Web. The course has lecture videos, learning activities like interactive concept quizzes, problem sets that can be completed on your own, answer sets to check your responses, problem-solving video help sessions taught by MIT teaching assistants, lists of important terms and definitions, suggested topics and links for further study, and exams with solution keys. These are structured in a clear and explicit way with a clear statement of learning objectives, a lecture video, a check yourself test and then another video with a check yourself test, before doing a set of practice problems to embed the information and skills, a list of further studies, and extra useful links that give other examples and applications. The whole session is embedded in a previous/next lecture series.

But that is not all. Running down the left hand side of the Web page is a social sharing site where students can join study groups, post questions and responses, and join the community of learners using the courses. If you are active on the open study group site you get rated and rewarded for your answers to questions. I joined the Foundations of Biology study group and was, as of 7 November 2012, a hatchling, with a zero smart score, zero problem solving and zero team work. The other person online was Sam who had a 99% smart rating, with 71% for team work (for helping 641 students, 438 of whom became fans), 99% for problem solving (answered 2 835 questions and received 1 074 medals) and 64% for engagement (studied for 240 days). Other universities like Stanford, Yale, Harvard and Berkeley also have open ware sites. We are back with the Salman Khan model, except that now whole universities are engaging in the project.

With the massive expansion of open courseware, it was only a matter of time before someone came up with an app for it and this is what Irynsoft has done. The idea is simple: turn your smartphone into a virtual classroom by pulling together and making available the open ware lectures provided by reputable institutions such as MIT and Stanford on your phone. While you participate in the course, you can google elements and issues and make notes, all on your phone while sitting on the bus. The company has a similar app specifically for the Khan Academy and for MIT open course ware. You have a genuine opportunity to learn whole courses over semesters and years. You might not get the degree and you do need to be able to afford a smart phone or have a computer with access to the Internet, all of which are serious issues. But such a monumental opening of sophisticated, organised knowledge and skills at the highest of academic levels has to be celebrated, even if its early incarnations result in massive drop out rates. If it's easy to access then it's easy to leave.

It's not only knowledge that is becoming more accessible – the technology to design and manage the process of making these courses is also simplifying and becoming more user-friendly all the time. Competing with big universities and companies designing these online courses are individuals at home, with a computer, resulting in an online explosion of systematic introductions to all the knowledges of the world. You can find my own cottage industry attempt to introduce education at www.waynehugo.co.za – one of them being an online introduction of this book.

Chapter 7

Conclusion: exercising the educational imagination

We have reached a point where we can take a breath, turn back and survey where we have travelled. Starting from one school we expanded outwards to view the collective material reality of all the schools of the world; then we contracted into the school itself and explored how its classrooms, furniture and equipment have changed over the last two centuries. Next, we jumped from the outer material world of the school into the individual material world of a child, using a micro switchover point of desk and learner, and investigated the smallest functioning units of learning (working memory). We then shifted to the inner depths of a student and explored the possible levels of development for which a student could reach. After outlining this interior world of an individual student we turned to how we learn collectively as a species, using the work of Piaget and Spencer to track across from individual to species learning. We finally went into the intricacies of constructing knowledge in pedagogically worthwhile ways, starting with the combination of basic elements and expanding outwards until we reached a point where it has become possible to access pedagogically most of the knowledge of the world at almost any time and in almost any space with a small device held in the hand, and now playing straight across our retinas through glasses.

Two organising activities guided this process of exercising our educational imaginations: climbing and jumping. I continually asked myself and you what the smallest educational units were and then expanded them outwards and upwards until the largest and highest units were reached. At the same time, I persistently shifted between different educational landscapes, jumping from the bricks and mortar of schools into brains and minds, interior depths, human species, knowledge forms, computer programs and virtual worlds. By working with dramatic scale, centuries of time and shifting panoramas (but always keeping an educational focus), the educational imagination starts to break out of its locatedness and begins to wonder.

The nature of climbing changed with the type of landscape. The material world works with expansion in scale and the logic of parts and wholes. This is very different from the functioning of material brains, the expansion of the interior world of the mind, and the development of species knowledge. The development of pedagogically structured knowledge happens in ways different from the material growth of schools; and the internal development of an individual is both related to and different from the collective development of our species.

The divisions causing the jumps are not easy to combine analytically and have been dramatised rather than theorised in this book. Inside/outside, one/many, virtual/actual, simple/complex, particular/general, old/new, concrete/abstract, body/mind, individual/collective, part/whole, micro/macro, homogenous/heterogonous (the list could go on) – all have massive debates on their own. The intention of this book was not to specialise in debates around the intersection of brain/mind, inside/outside and individual/collective, but to develop your educational imagination. At the same time a basic structure for the complex field of education studies was provided to make sense of the working of education in all its complex glory.

So if we step back from the flow of the book, what can we say about the operating principles of the educational imagination and the basic structure of education studies?

The first point is to recognise the necessity of working with scales, much as musicians do, running up and down the notes, making sure that each is distinct but also located in a range. If it's a spatial focus in education then try to locate the smallest and largest elements and all the levels in between. If it's time then work from earliest to what is most recent and upcoming; if it's complexity move from simplest to most complex; if it's moral development start with what is most elementary and move to what is most profound; and if it's intellectual development begin with the most basic of links and reach for the most subtle and delicate of abstractions. One of the reasons why intellectuals like Plato, Aristotle, Dante, Hegel, Spencer, Piaget, Kohlberg, Maslow, Bronfenbrenner, Gagné and Bernstein are celebrated is because they have charted paths that move across astonishing distances in ways that show us how to walk the same path. Plato took us from the dark cave of everyday experience into the light of abstraction. Aristotle showed us how to classify all of existence from its most general categories to its most specific. Dante took us all the way from the depths of hell to the heights of heaven. Hegel opened out the dialectical development of full consciousness by taking us on a journey through the history of Western philosophy. Spencer opened out the development of existence from homogeneity to heterogeneity. Piaget told the story of our individual development from sensorimotor perception to formal operational thinking and then folded this into the development of species knowledge. Kohlberg revealed the moral dimensions of a similar journey. Maslow opened out the full potential of development within us from physiological needs to transcendence. Bronfenbrenner showed us how to travel from micro, through meso, to macro and chrono. Gagné worked through the steps travelled to make a skill understandable and do-able. And Bernstein opened out the full range an educational message travels from its esoteric formulation in the sacred heights to its pedagogic articulation and assessment in the practicalities of classroom life.

There is much to dispute over the accuracy and legitimacy of these accounts and the engagement with the truth-values of the different types of journeys cannot be ignored. But the reason why someone like Dante is celebrated, even though his medieval poem now reads like a wild rant on acid, is because of the sheer reach of the verse, able to express poetically the experience of travelling to the darkest depths of depravity, through the disciplines of purgatory and into the heights of the sacred, recounted step by step, circle by circle, level by level. Something of this flavour pervades the book (I hope). But even with Dante's enormous capacity, he draws a boundary around what he does and then sticks to it, carefully, rigorously and timeously. The journey from hell through purgatory to heaven takes three days, each sub-journey told in 33 cantos (with an extra introduction for the Inferno), each line of the canto following a set logic of rhyme and meter. There is a bottom point, where the lowest level of hell is reached. This has to be identified, described, swung through so that the climb upwards can begin. Just so for the end point in the highest of high heavens, clearly delineated so that the journey can end.

The educational imagination has also to work with these logics. There is a point where what is education stops and something else takes over and this is often one of the most difficult lines to identify, because interlinked and meshed processes are being looked at. This is why we started the book with a boundary that was easy to see – that of a physical school. With the shift to an individual student, the boundaries become far harder to identify, the line between what is neurological and educational being exceptionally hard to chart as we saw in chapter 3, but it is important to try to locate it, otherwise one travels into fascinating regions outside the ambit of education and increasingly less relevant to its concerns. A similar problem is reached with the shift from individual to species, and from what is inside an individual to what is outside, where issues of biology, language, culture, family, state and economic development all come into play. This book does not pretend to theorise these boundary lines, or negotiate how different types of boundaries intersect, overlap and laminate. What it tries to do is show what happens when there is a driving concern to stay within the educational, but push it to its limits.

The second point to note is that the key driver of the educational imagination, rather than a poetic, social or divine imagination, is reflective abstraction. When I read Piaget I am blown away by the imaginative reach of the man, but what stays with me is his precise articulation of what reflective abstraction is and then his demonstration of how it plays out, both in the intellectual development of an individual and the collective knowledge of the species. It irks me when I encounter summary after summary of his stages in educational textbooks without due accord given to his profound articulation of the driving mechanism behind the educational imagination. It is in the struggle of reflective abstraction to *expand the reach of the possible as it comes closer and closer towards the fullness of reality* that we have the educational equivalent to Dante's *Divine Comedy*. Reflective abstraction reduces the gap between the possible and the necessary by increasing the range and sophistication of the possible, enabling it to get closer and closer to the fullness of reality; and it is education's role to induct us into the realm of how the possible gets closer to the actual through knowledge, all the while recognising just how massively beautiful the actual is. *Boundaries of the Educational Imagination* does this by stretching the possible out to its largest, highest, furthest reaches so that it gets close to full taste of real education in all its magnitude and richness.

As you practise the scales of education, a discriminatory ability develops that identifies different domains within a broad area. We saw this with Piaget and his levels of intellectual development, where Demetriou pointed to different streams of reasoning going on inside the broader field of intellectual development such as categorical, quantitative, spatial, causal, social and verbal. Being able to recognise domains is a little like becoming increasingly able to play chords as scales, where four of five notes are all struck at the same time, each separate, but part of the same structure. In effect what you try to develop is an ability to travel through levels while attending to different streams that run through the levels in distinctive ways, sometimes harmonising, sometimes conflicting as in figure 7.1.

As your educational imagination strengthens, you can begin to attend to the dissimilarities between different types of movement through levels. For example, as one shifts from micro to macro what happens is that space grows bigger and bigger. But what happens to space when one shifts from concrete to abstract? The concrete particular is located in space, but as one shifts into increasingly abstract formulations, the nature of location in space moves to some weird other non-concrete conceptual space. The way you work with levels that go from micro to macro is very different from the way you work with levels that go from concrete to abstract. The same can be said for going from part to whole, simple to complex, the particular to the general, everyday to the specialised and the homogenous to the heterogeneous.

Each of these processes works with levels, but in very different ways. To be frank, when I started writing this book it was with the intention of making explicit how these different types of level intersect with each other, and how each has many varieties contained within them, but I quickly realised that another book needed to be written before this articulation was possible. I did not want to kill off my own attempt to stimulate the educational imagination by providing too heavy a meal, so this book attempted a lighter path that settled on taking a journey through the different types of levels and showing how the educational imagination plays with them. A later book I am in the process of conceptualising – *Advanced Educational Analysis* – will not step back from the struggle to fully articulate these processes with more rigour and weight.

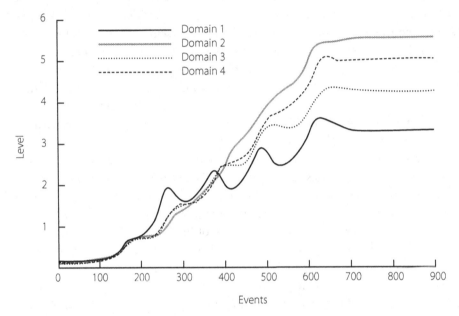

Figure 7.1 Spreading pattern of hierarchical development

Boundaries of the Educational Imagination does not only play with scales, it also worked with juxtapositions: an old slate tablet with an iPad; old school chairs and desks with new school chairs and desks; paper fibres with brain fibres; and Carter High School in comparison to Mpande High School. When the imagination works with juxtapositions, the first thing it does is get the two input spaces into some kind of equivalence and then look for connections between them.

This particular function of the educational imagination develops as one stays within particular levels of focus and travels around a bit. With the tablet example, one of the oldest elements within the materiality of learning was juxtaposed with the most recent. Centuries were jumped over while keeping constant what it is students hold in their hands. If you are interested in developing this particular aspect of the educational imagination in more detail, my edited book *Conceptual Integration and Educational Analysis* (HSRC Press, 2015) will provide detailed examples of how to do it along with its operating principles.

If levels above and below the current level of focus provide a clear training ground for stretching the educational imagination, and juxtapositions from the travels provide a startling richness, then it is in working with combinations of variables that the educational imagination develops an ability to work with variation. The hard work needed at this point is practice at the possible combinations, running them through the imagination: what happens if I combine this variable with that variable and then add this one in this way? How does it differ from combining the variables in a different way? Our educational imaginations are often entranced by one picture of good education, and then become entrapped, especially if the picture is called something that has an imaginative ring to it. The entrapment works when the picture itself is the name for a creative and imaginative process, so we imagine that by insisting on its implementation across the world we are furthering creativity and imagination everywhere we go. By insisting on one way of teaching, like progressivism or learner-centred education, we feel that we are enriching the whole educational world when what we are actually doing is repeating one stuck move over and over again. The educational imagination has to be able to work with all the possible varieties of education, different types of curriculum, pedagogy and assessment, and with various types of relationship between teachers and students. If you are interested in developing this particular aspect of the educational imagination in more detail, then read the sister work to this book, *Cracking the Code to Educational Analysis* (2013).[29]

Cracking the Code teaches the educational imagination to work with variation; *Boundaries of the Educational Imagination* teaches the educational imagination to travel through levels; *Conceptual Integration* teaches the educational imagination how to juxtapose and blend different elements within these travels. Combined, these three books provide the elementary practices of a combinatorial matrix, playing of scales and juxtaposition; enabling travelling through the depths, heights and abundance of education, and always paying attention to where it starts and ends.

I have pointed out two uses of this book: first to develop the educational imagination; and second to provide an underlying structure by which the complex world of education opened out for study. This book is a primer for education studies. In no way is it meant to replace the complex dynamics of education studies that involves a combination of history, sociology, psychology, philosophy, economics, linguistics, geography and politics.

The combination of different disciplines makes education studies one of the most exciting of fields because all of the human sciences are relevant to it. Education studies provides you with a licence to explore the whole world precisely because education is intimately wrapped up in what it is to be human. This dynamic is what brought me out of my own intellectual slumber at university. Education studies presented me with an opportunity to explore the full range of the human sciences with the proviso that it held educational relevance. It still excites me. We have failed miserably to live up to this tradition in our current textbooks on education studies.

It is, and should be, one of the most exciting areas of study that exposes students to the beauty and tragedy of education. The problem for a beginner student, and even for lecturers in the field, is that the complexity results in enormous confusion around what actually to do in the subject. How do you cover history of education, sociology of education, psychology of education, philosophy of education, economics of education, politics of education, geography of education and linguistics of education while trying to get students to understand how pedagogy, curriculum, assessment and policy operate in conditions of inequality?

This book does not attempt to do the above, but what it does do is provide a primer to education studies by simplifying the complexity through two distinctions – collective/individual and material/interior; and one rule – climb through the respective levels until they lose educational relevance.

Let's start with the basic distinction between individual and collective. Crudely put, studies that focus on the individual dimension are psychological and studies that focus on the collective dimension are sociological (figure 7.2).

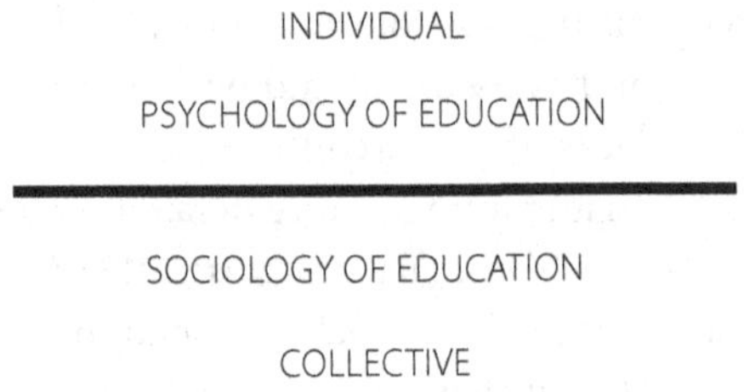

INDIVIDUAL

PSYCHOLOGY OF EDUCATION

SOCIOLOGY OF EDUCATION

COLLECTIVE

Figure 7.2 Distinction between individual and collective

Interrogations of how this distinction actually works and whether it is valid partly make up the field of philosophy. What does it mean to be an individual; to be a part of a collective; does the collective not produce individuals; are collectives not actually made up of individuals? What is the nature of a boundary? Questioning the nature of the concepts and the validity of the distinctions is the work of philosophy of education (figure 7.3).

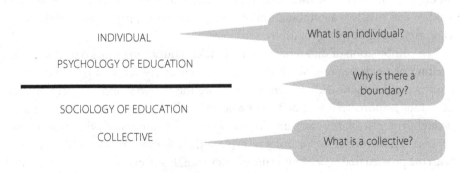

Figure 7.3 Philosophy clarifies and questions boundaries

The issue with psychology of education is that part of it focuses on the development of our interior and another on the functioning of our bodies, especially our brain. We have internal accounts of the development of our minds and external accounts of how our bodies are stimulus response mechanisms (Pavlov and Skinner), or how our brains function neurologically (figure 7.4).

The key point is not to get stuck in an either/or mentality where you write off studies on the body or brain of a student because they are too positivist or behaviourist. There are issues to do with overly simplistic behaviourist accounts, but that should force you to look for *better* accounts of material individuality rather than replace it with more interior, interpretive, qualitative accounts. Stay within a quadrant and look for more up-to-date accounts that push beyond Pavlov and Skinner for example. Don't simplistically dismiss Skinner and behaviourism and replace him with Piaget and Vygotsky. You risk leaving out a whole quadrant by writing off its early or crude versions.

A similar set of distinctions and patterns holds for sociology, with more material accounts emphasising tangible collective inequalities that can be seen (black and white, male and female, rich and poor) and more interior accounts emphasising how language, culture and meaning work at an interior collective dimension (figure 7.5). Material differences take us into the world of economic and geographic inequality. Symbolic differences take us into the world of cultural capital, more symbolic types of violence and restricted and elaborated linguistic codes.

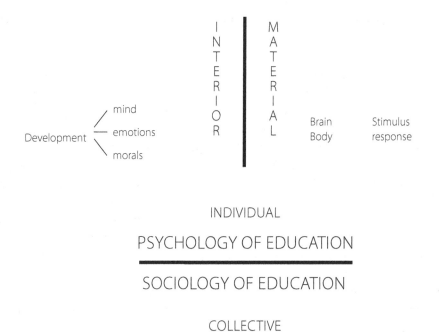

Figure 7.4 Individual domain can be divided into interior and material sections

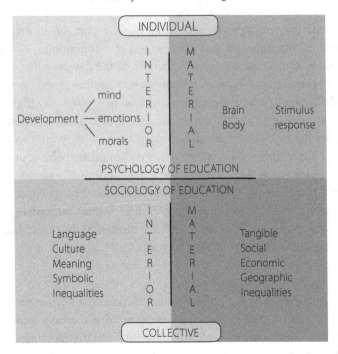

Figure 7.5 The collective domain can be divided into interior and material domains

Of late, with the massive rise to popularity of post-modernism there has been a strong focus on symbolic meaning, often at the cost of material inequalities and realities. What you have to watch out for are radical positions that explain everything in education through a single domain. This is surprisingly common, with some arguing that our learning is basically explained by how the brain works. Others argue that education only makes sense when put in the context of class struggle, or that it is the mind of an individual learner that constructs all of reality; while some point to social interaction as providing the secret key to understanding education. We can visually catch these dreams of omnipotence in figures 7.6 to 7.9.

It's one thing to make your area of specialisation the most important aspect of your professional life; another to project it as the answer to all of education's problems.

Just as bad are trite forms of integral holism where everything counts and you can get away with an 'it's complex' line, where as many factors as possible are thrown together into a mushy, sloppy soup. There is real hard work in deducing how the brain and mind interact, social and psychological factors inter-relate, and social structure and social meaning interdepend; how the outside becomes the inside, and the inside the outside. These are some of the hardest questions that currently face us. Piaget was one of the most gifted polymaths of the twentieth century who spent decades attempting to master the human and natural sciences to understand how we learn, working between individual and collective forms of learning knowledge, and between our physical and interior adaptation mechanisms. All of it was a mystery to him and certainly a simple four quadrants with a climbing mechanism inside each would not have solved any of his problems.

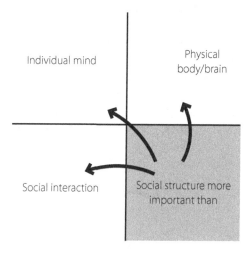

Figure 7.6   *Social structural explanation dominates*

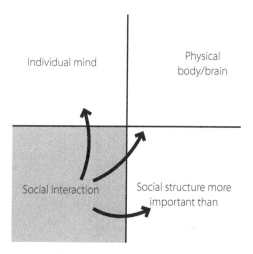

Figure 7.7 *Social interaction explanation dominates*

But we all have to start somewhere, so I have written this book as a start-up. There is merit in trying to make a starting point as simple as possible while still getting at the essential structure and that is what I tried to do by making two elementary distinctions and then travelling around in the spaces they produced. I did not interrogate the nature of the distinctions, the difficulties of boundary crossings, or the way the spaces are intimately tied up with each other. I don't want to leave you with an oversimplified comment that all the quadrants work together in a complex way, or that they give you everything you need to imagine the varieties of educational experience. This book is a primer. It prepares the surface for the study of education and puts in place a small amount of dynamite so that the main explosive event can happen. It is a first book of elementary distinctions that enables the educational imagination to begin its travels. It is written for someone interested in the way the study of education works. It provides two simple distinctions between individual/collective and material/interior to make sense of it all; and a basic rule that helps an education student to climb through its basic levels and not get lost by travelling too far into the worlds of psychology, sociology, philosophy, economics, linguistics, geography, politics and other human sciences.

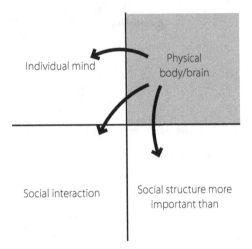

Figure 7.8 Physical body/brain explanation dominates

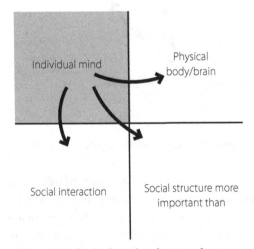

Figure 7.9 Individual mind explanation dominates

This forces a half apology from me. Although *Boundaries of the Educational Imagination* stands in its own right as an introductory primer to the educational imagination, it is best used with *Cracking the Code* and *Conceptual Integration*. Here comes the other half of the apology. In no way do these three texts and the practices contained in them provide the educational imagination with everything it needs to function. A playing of educational scales, a combinatorial matrix of education variables and the metaphoric combination of different inputs do amazing things for the development of an educational imagination, but none provide an ethical heartland that gives the grounding principles behind why we educate and are so passionate about it. A full educational imagination is able to do more than recognise different possible variations of educational experience, walk through its assorted levels and conceptually blend different inputs. It is able to negotiate the ethical principles that sit behind matrices and levels and light them up from a deep backdrop. More than this, it should be able to imagine how different ethical principles operate in different ways and politically negotiate a path through them depending on the situation at hand. But that is to anticipate *The Good Fight*, to which I now turn.

References

The Black Board in the Primary School: A Manual for Teachers. (1841). Boston: Perkins and Marvis.

Bringuier, J.C. (1980). *Conversations With Jean Piaget.* Chicago: University of Chicago Press.

British and Foreign School Society. (1816). *Manual of the System of the British and Foreign School Society of London, for Teaching Reading, Writing, Arithmetic, and Needle-work, in the Elementary Schools.* London: Longman.

Burke, C. and Grosvenor, I. (2008). *School.* London: Reaktion Books.

Chase, W.G. and Simon, H.A. (1973). 'The mind's eye in chess' in *Visual Information Processing* edited by W.G. Chase. New York: Academic Press, pp. 215–281.

Chen, C.M. (2009). 'Ontology-based concept map for planning a personalized learning path'. *British Journal of Educational Technology* 40(6), pp. 1028–1058.

Cooper, G. (1998). An Introduction to Applications of Cognitive Load Theory to Instructional Design. A presentation at the Education 1998 Conference.

Criticos, C. (undated). *Learning Spaces Development in Southern Africa.* Pietermaritzburg: Mimeo.

D'Anna, C.A., Zechmeister, E.B. and Hall, J.W. (1991). 'Toward a meaningful definition of vocabulary size'. *Journal of Literacy Research* 23, pp. 109–122.

De Gregori, A. (2011). *Reimagining the Classroom: Opportunities to Link Recent Advances in Pedagogy to Physical Settings.* Available at http://mcgraw-hillresearchfoundation.org/wp-content/uploads/2011/10/Reimagining_the_Classroom_DeGregoriFINAL.pdf.

De Groot, A.D. (1965). *Thought and Choice in Chess.* The Hague: Mouton Publishers.

Demetriou, A., Spanoudis, G. and Mouyi, A. (2010). 'A three-level model of the developing mind: functional and neuronal substantiation' in *The Developmental Relations Between Mind, Brain, and Education: Essays in Honor of Robbie Case* edited by M. Ferrari and L. Vuletic. New York: Springer.

Dennehy, S. (2009). 'The design of school furniture for primary school children' in *Irish Ergonomics Review: Proceedings of the Irish Ergonomics Society Annual Conference 2009* edited by L.W. O'Sullivan. Dublin: Irish Ergonomics Society.

Efron, B. and Thisted, R. (1976). 'Estimating the number of unseen species: how many words did Shakespeare know?' *Biometrika* 63(3), pp. 435–447.

Egan, K. (2002). *Getting it Wrong from the Beginning: Our Progressivist Inheritance from Herbert Spencer, John Dewey, and Jean Piaget.* New Haven: Yale University Press.

Gagné, Robert M. et al. (1962). 'Factors in acquiring knowledge of a mathematical task' in *Psychological Monographs: General and Applied* 76(7), pp. 1-21.

Gould, S.J. (1977). *Ontogeny and Phylogeny.* Cambridge, MA: Belknap Press.

Hall, N. (2003). 'The role of the slate in Lancasterian schools as evidenced by their manuals and handbooks'. *Paradigm* 2(7), pp. 46–54.

Herman, F. et al. (2011). 'The school desk: from concept to object'. *History of Education* 40(1), pp. 97–117.

Horan, B., Gardner, M. and Scott, J. (2009). *MiRTLE: A Mixed Reality Teaching and Learning Environment.* Technical report UMI Order Number: SERIES13103. Sun Microsystems.

Hugo, W. (2007). *Ladders of Beauty: Hierarchical Pedagogy from Plato to Dante.* Berne: Peter Lang.

Hugo, W. (2013). *Cracking the Code to Educational Analysis.* Cape Town: Pearson.

Hugo, W. (forthcoming, 2015). *Conceptual Integration and Educational Analysis.* Cape Town: HSRC Press.

Jones, B.F. (2010). 'Age and great invention'. *Review of Economics and Statistics* 92(1), pp.1–14.

Kalra, P. and O'Keefe, J.K. (2011). 'Communication in mind, brain, and education: making disciplinary differences explicit'. *Mind, Brain and Education* 5(4), pp. 163–171.

Khan, S. (2012). *The One World Schoolhouse: Education Reimagined.* London: Hodder and Stoughton.

Kirschner, P. A., Sweller, J. and Clark, R. E. (2006). 'Why minimal guidance during instruction does not work: an analysis of the failure of constructivist, discovery, problem-based experiential and inquiry-based teaching'. *Educational Psychologist* 41(2), pp. 75–86.

Lancaster, J. (1810). *The British System of Education.* London: Longman.

Lewin, K. M. (2008). *Strategies for Sustainable Financing of Secondary Education in Sub-Saharan Africa.* Washington: World Bank. Available at https://openknowledge.worldbank.org/handle/10986/6389.

Lewin, K. M. and Sabates, R. (2012). 'Who gets what?: is improved access to basic education pro-poor in sub-Saharan Africa?' *International Journal of Educational Development* 32(4), pp. 517–528.

Marx, K. (1852). 'The eighteenth Brumaire of Louis Bonaparte' in *Karl Marx: A*

Reader by J. Elster. Cambridge: Cambridge University Press.

Maslow, A. H. (1968). *Toward a Psychology of Being*. New York: Van Nostrand.

Maslow, A.H. (1971). *The Farther Reaches of Human Nature*. New York: Viking.

Menzel, P. and D'Aluisio, F. (2007). *Hungry Planet: What the World Eats*. New York: Random House.

Menzel, P., Mann, C.C. and Kennedy, P. (1994). *Material World: Global Family Portrait*. Berkeley: University of California Press.

Mesoudi, A. (2011). 'Variable cultural acquisition costs constrain cumulative cultural evolution'. *PLoS ONE* 6(3): e18239.

Miller, G.A. (1956). 'The magical number seven, plus or minus two: some limits on our capacity for processing information' *Psychological Review* 63(2): 81−97.

Miller, P. (2004). 'Gender and education before and after mass schooling' in *A Companion to Gender History* edited by T.A. Meade and Merry E. Wiesner-Hanks. Oxford: Blackwell, pp. 129−145

Mohamedbhai, G. (2009). *Effects of Massification on Higher Education in Africa, 2008*. Accra: Association of African Universities.

Nethengwe, M.E. (2008). *Traditional and Alternative Views of the Performance of Provincial School Systems in South Africa*. Masters Thesis: International Institute for Educational Planning.

Paivio, A. (1986). *Mental Representations: A Dual Coding Approach*. New York: Oxford University Press.

Parsons, T. (2009). *Thinking: Objects: Contemporary Approaches to Product Design*. Lausanne: AVA Publishing.

Perry, W. G. (1970). *Forms of Intellectual and Ethical Development in the College Years: A Scheme*. New York: Holt, Rinehart and Winston.

Piaget, J. (1970). *Genetic Epistemology* translated by Eleanor Duckworth. New York: Columbia University Press.

Richey, Rita (ed.). (2000). *The Legacy of Robert M. Gagné*. Syracuse, N.Y.: ERIC Clearinghouse on Information and Technology.

Robson, E.R. (1874). *School Architecture*. London: John Murray.

Rose, L.T. and Fischer, K.W. (2009). 'Dynamic development: a neo-Piagetian approach' in *The Cambridge Companion to Piaget* edited by U. Muller, J. Carpendale and L. Smith. Cambridge: Cambridge University Press, pp. 400−421.

Samir, K.C., Barakat, B., Goujon, A., Skirbekk, V., Sanderson W., Lutz W. (2010). 'Projection of populations by level of educational attainment, age and sex for 120 countries for 2005−2050'. *Demographic Research* 22(15), pp. 383−472.

Shell, D.F. et al. (2010). *The Unified Learning Model: How Motivational, Cognitive and Neurobiological Sciences Inform Best Teaching Practices*. Dordrecht: Springer.

Smart, B. (2003). 'Ontology' in *Blackwell Guide to the Philosophy of Computing and Information* edited by L. Floridi. Oxford: Blackwell, pp. 155−166.

Spaull, N. (2011). 'A preliminary analysis of SACMEQ III South Africa'. *Stellenbosch Economic Working Papers* 11/11.

Spaull, N. (2012). 'Poverty and privilege: primary school inequality in South Africa'. *Stellenbosch Economic Working Papers* 13/12.

Spencer, H. (1857). 'Progress: its law and cause'. *Westminster Review* 67, pp. 445–485.

Spencer, H. (1861). *Education: Intellectual, Moral and Physical*. London: Williams and Norgate.

Spencer, H. (1862). *First Principles*. London: Williams and Norgate.

Spencer, H. (1882–1898). *The Principles of Sociology*. 3 vols. London: Williams and Norgate.

Sudjic, D. and Brown, L. (1988). *The Modern Chair*. London: Institute of Contemporary Arts.

Sweller, J., Kirschner, P.A. and Clark, R.E. (2007). 'Why minimally guided teaching techniques do not work: a reply to commentaries'. *Educational Psychologist* 42(2), pp. 115–121.

Sweller, J., van Merriënboer, J.J.G. and Paas, F. (1998). 'Cognitive architecture and instructional design'. *Educational Psychology Review* 10, pp. 252–296.

Tobler, W. (1970). 'A computer movie simulating urban growth in the Detroit region'. *Economic Geography* 46, pp. 234–240.

Wilber, K. (2000). *Sex, Ecology, Spirituality: The Spirit of Evolution*. 2nd revised edition. Boston: Shambhala.

Wilber, K. (2007). *A Brief History of Everything*. 2nd edition. Boston: Shambhala.

Willingham, D.T. (2004). 'Reframing the mind: Howard Gardner and the theory of multiple intelligences'. *Education Next* 4(3), pp. 19–24.

Willingham, D.T. (2009). 'Three problems in the marriage of neuroscience and education'. *Cortex* 45, pp. 54–55.

Willingham, D.T. and Lloyd, J.W. (2007). 'How educational theories can use neuroscientific data'. *Mind, Brain and Education* 1(3), pp. 140–149.

Endnotes

1   There are complications and caveats to this simple picture. Many countries in the South are on a strong upward developmental path, like the BRICS countries; while some countries in the North are on a strong downward path, like Greece and possibly Italy and Spain. Others have become failed states or descended into war. Take a look at the table below. It is based on a fascinating attempt by the United Nations to rank all the countries of the world on a human development index (HDI). At http://hdr.undp.org/en/statistics/ you will find an excellent website that uses three basic dimensions (health, education and income) to rank countries from best to worst on a HDI. I selected seven countries, the five BRICS and the highest and lowest country. The bold figures are final scores based on a combination of key indicators in each component (for education it consists of indicators like public expenditure, expected years of schooling of children, adult literacy rate and mean years of schooling of adults). The bottom figure in brackets provides one key indicator inside each component.

Rank	Country	Health (life expectancy)	Education (mean years of education)	Income (US dollars per year)	HDI
1	Norway	**96.4** (81.1 years)	**98.5** (12.6 years)	**88.3** ($47 557)	**94.3**
66	Russia	**77.0** (68.8 years)	**78.4** (9.8 years)	**71.3** ($14 561)	**75.5**
84	Brazil	**84.4** (73.5 years)	**66.3** (7.2 years)	**66.2** ($10 162)	**71.8**

Rank	Country	Health (life expectancy)	Education (mean years of education)	Income (US dollars per year)	HDI
101	China	84.3 (73.5 years)	62.3 (7.5 years)	61.8 ($7 476)	68.7
123	South Africa	51.7 (52.8 years)	70.5 (8.5 years)	65.2 ($9 469)	61.9
134	India	71.7 (65.4 years)	45 (4.4 years)	50.8 ($3 468)	54.7
187	Democratic Republic of Congo	44.8 (48.4 years)	35.6 (3.5 years)	14.7 ($280)	28.6

Each country has a different education story to tell and we shall explore a country level focus later on in this chapter, but the key point is that there are other organising logics that run in complex parallels with education.

2   http://www.sacmeq.org/visualization-research.htm.

3   The Southern and Eastern Consortium for Monitoring Education Quality (SACMEQ) has conducted three projects across the region in the last few decades. The first (SACMEQ 1) ran from 1995 to 1998, the second from 1998 to 2004 and the third from 2005 to 2010, with the numbers of students, teachers and schools increasing each time. SACMEQ I involved seven countries, 20 000 learners and 1 000 primary schools; SACMEQ II had 40 000 learners, 5 300 teachers and 2 000 primary schools; and SACMEQ III studied 15 countries with 61 000 learners, 8 000 teachers and around 2 700 schools (Spaull, 2011, p. 40). There are problems with the validity of the tests as the South African versions were available only in English and Afrikaans, thus putting most students at a disadvantage to other countries testing in home languages.

4   http://www.sacmeq.org/visualization-research.htm.

5   http://www.unesco.org/new/en/education/about-us/how-we-work/mission/.

6   http://huebler.blogspot.com/2012_07_01_archive.html.

7   This open-access work is published under the terms of the Creative Commons Attribution Non-Commercial License 2.0 Germany, which permits use, reproduction and distribution in any medium for non-commercial purposes, provided the original author(s) and source are given credit. See http://creativecommons.org/licenses/by-nc/2.0/de/.

8   This does not mean that mass education only began in the nineteenth century, but Tau would not have been able to see it clearly from above. After the Reformation there was a concerted attempt in Scandinavian countries to ensure literacy for Christian purposes, but this was done inside homes with tests in the parish (Miller, 2006, p. 131).

9   Feminisation of teaching varied by country (Miller, 2004). In Denmark and Germany, for example, it has been far slower than other European countries.

10 http://www.unesco.org/new/en/education/themes/leading-the-international-agenda/gender-and-education/resources/the-world-atlas-of-gender-equality-in-education/.

11 The idea of a one-room schoolhouse has not disappeared, especially from the mind-sets of progressive educators who are attracted to the idea of everyone living together as one big happy family. The Discovery Charter School in Newark, New Jersey, has attempted just such a model. Here is a description by De Gregori:

> Walking past the attended entrance room, the visitor is immediately introduced to a vast scenario. Here, students from different grades sit at small, individual, easily movable tables, forming groups around their teachers. Student tables and other elements are painted in various bright colours, and they become purposeful, cost-effective components of the larger classroom space, contributing to its vitality. A variety of plants are also installed in the room, providing a link between the man-made and natural environments. The room, occasionally divided with a few transferable low partitions, is full of activity. There are students sitting, reading and writing at workstations along the walls. Laptops are noticeable, but not as much as voices. Questions and answers fly across the room. It could be described as a choral humming interspersed with solos. However, the noise and movement of people appear not to distract from the various learning activities (De Gregori, 2011, p. 9).

12 It still took the Germans another 120 years to get to the point where over three quarters of their children were in school. Developing countries in Africa have been given far less time to attempt the same feat and without the benefits of colonial plunder to help them.

13 Robson was being a little unfair. There were specific technical and architectural discussions about the optimum size and shape of schoolrooms in England (see British and Foreign School Society, 1816, pp. 3–5).

14 http://www.virtualclassrooms.info/machinima.htm.

15 http://www.ascilite.org.au/ajet/ajet28/gregory1.jpg.

16 http://www.simschool.org/about.

17 https://moodle.org/stats/.

18 See www.functionalfate.org for a dedicated website.

19 Semantic knowledge is further divided into declarative and procedural knowledge: the difference being the ability to say what you know and do what you know. It's a foundational distinction, especially in education, but at one level too fine for a book as introductory as this one. It has been hard for me as a writer to make decisions about where to cut off the level of focus.

This is not due to engaging in fields that lose their educational purchase, but because the level is too fine for a primer. The choice not to go into more detail about how cognitive science classifies knowledge is particularly tough as the full set of distinctions provides a powerful map of how we work with knowledge in education. But it's simply too hard to carry both intricate detail and an introduction to the broad terrain at the same time. For example, here is a more complex figure of working memory:

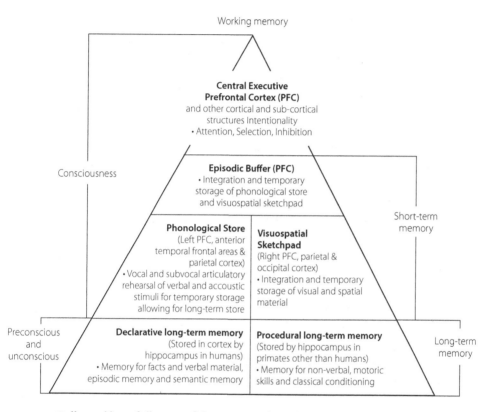

Followed by a fuller set of distinctions than the ones I work with in this chapter.

20 Go to http://www.youtube.com/watch?v=vJG698U2Mvo.

21 He had a terrible relationship with his mother and blamed it partly on her lack of purchase on reality. As he noted, 'I have always detested any departure from reality, an attitude which I relate to my mother's poor mental health'.

22 http://camsacar.files.wordpress.com/2009/05/zeno_paradox.gif.

23 This account is based on the research of Perry, who conducted in-depth interviews with undergraduate students at Harvard during the 1960s. Neither Harvard nor the 1960s are representative of what is happening to students across the world, nor does development stop with undergraduates: what of postgraduates and the much needed critique of relativism?

24 Biologists used the way we learn as an analogy for how we work at a

molecular level that strangely mimics what is now used in cognitive science. The reason why we speed up going through the stages is that each generation practises it and becomes more adept (Gould, 1977, p. 100).

25 Piaget, like Spencer, was a polymath interested in finding a theory of everything and, like Spencer, felt the answer revolves around how parts work with wholes: 'I suddenly understood that at all levels (viz. that of living cells, organism, species, society, etc.) but also with reference to states of conscience, to concepts, to logical principles, etc. one finds the same problem of the relationship between the parts and the whole; hence I was convinced I had found the solution.' Like Spencer, Piaget felt that the way parts and wholes interacted gave him the golden key to an understanding of all existence. But contrary to Spencer, Piaget sensed that the individual child could be used to understand the whole species, not in terms of biological recapitulation, but how the emergence of knowledge in the individual child would reveal the emergence of knowledge in the human species. Rather than use the part/whole relation as a metaphysical doctrine, he set out to understand how a child works with parts and wholes, and in so doing uncovered a whole new world we are still exploring.

26 https://www.khanacademy.org/about/the-team.

27 http://www.teacherspayteachers.com/Product/Learning-ar-with-Pirate-Mark-r-controlled-vowels.

28 7.01SC Fundamentals of Biology, Fall 2011. Massachusetts Institute of Technology: MIT OpenCourseWare, http://ocw.mit.edu (Accessed 7 November 2012). License: Creative Commons BY-NC-SA.

29 You are welcome to do my introductory online course on educational analysis. It's around five hours long and has questions throughout that give you immediate feedback. It is called 'Educational analysis for beginners' and you can find it here: http://zapt.io/tegmues. I keep track of all participants and get feedback on all your responses.

Printed in the United States
By Bookmasters